I NOW
PRONOUNCE YOU
FINANCIALLY

How to **PROTECT YOUR MONEY**
in **MARRIAGE** *and* **DIVORCE**

FIT

PAM FRIEDMAN, CFP®, CDFA®

RIVER GROVE
BOOKS

Published by River Grove Books
Austin, TX
www.rivergrovebooks.com

Distributed by River Grove Books

Design and composition by Greenleaf Book Group and Kim Lance
Cover design by Greenleaf Book Group and Kim Lance
Cover image: ©Thinkstock/MaksimKoval

Cataloging-in-Publication data is available.

Print ISBN: 978-1-63299-068-6

eBook ISBN: 978-1-63299-069-3

First Edition

With gratitude to my husband, Mitch,
and to Rebecca Sundet-Schoenwald,
for adding their support, talent,
and humor to the writing of this book.

Contents

Disclaimer

THIS BOOK IS DESIGNED TO PROVIDE accurate and authoritative information on the subject of money in marriage and divorce. All material presented is believed to be from sources that are reliable, and no representations are made as to another party's informational accuracy or completeness.

The opinions expressed herein are solely those of the Author unless otherwise specifically cited. It is understood that neither the Author nor the Publisher is engaged in rendering legal, accounting, or other professional services by publishing this book. As each individual situation is unique, questions relevant to personal finance and divorce specific to the individual or business should be addressed with an appropriate professional to ensure that the situation has been evaluated carefully and appropriately. The Author and Publisher specifically disclaim any liabilities, loss, or risk that is incurred as a consequence, directly or indirectly, of the use and application of any of the contents of this work.

All examples provided are used to demonstrate possible situations that individuals may need to address. The names provided are not real, and the situations have been enhanced to better demonstrate the potential pitfalls.

Introduction

"I WISH I HAD MET YOU before my divorce." I've heard that phrase so many times I should engrave it into a paperweight for my office. I hear it when I explain my line of work, whether I'm at a party, at a luncheon, or I just finished speaking at a conference or workshop.

Both men and women think marriage is supposed to be about trust, love, and romance. And they're right. But there's a reality they're ignoring: The current divorce rate is about 50 percent. People willingly enter into marriage without even glancing in reality's direction. They're not about to consider the laws regarding marriage and divorce when there are caterers to hire and dicey family dynamics to manage. They miss the opportunity to educate themselves about the impact of marriage and divorce on their money and on their children's well-being. There is a lingering taboo regarding divorce that causes people—financial planners included—to avoid this particular kind of planning.

The chapters ahead approach financial planning through the lens of relationships, in marriage and out. You'll get the same information I provide my clients, most of whom, unfortunately, find me after they've already hired and paid dearly for an attorney. They think they have a legal problem. "I wanted a divorce, so I called an attorney," they tell me. Financial realities quickly follow this knee-jerk reaction. You need both an attorney and a financial planner, and they need to be open to working together to get the best possible results.

This book helps you talk about and protect what you've earned—before, during, and after marriage. The first part covers premarriage and marital financial planning. You'll learn how emotion impacts financial decision making, how to start a conversation about money, why you might want a marital agreement, and how to prepare to negotiate and monitor one. You'll also learn new strategies to budget, save, and protect your money as a couple. If you've already decided to divorce, the second part of this book will help you preserve your money as you move forward in your divorce and in your life.

I want you to have the tools and knowledge to make the right choices with your money. By reading this book, you can benefit the way my clients have: You'll be able to use the strategies illustrated here to plan a secure financial future before you marry, while you're married, or if necessary, after your marriage ends.

1

The Ties that Bind

MONEY TALKS, BUT IT ALSO WALKS. Just like our husbands, wives, partners, and lovers. If we *listen* to our partners, and support and respect them, we're going a long way to keeping them. If we don't, our partners may leave us. Money requires attention, too. Deprived of care and respect, it departs, escorted away by ignorance and fear.

If only we understood that money is really just the grease that keeps the cogs of life's machinery moving smoothly, we would be able to avoid so many financial problems.

Instead we attach a range of emotions, real or imagined, to our money. After all, who hasn't heard the phrase: "Money is the root of all evil"? Who wants to talk about that?

But enough with metaphors and clichés. The fact is that money enables us to do things for ourselves, our partners, our parents, and our children that are otherwise impossible. That's why I'm a little mystified by most people's reluctance to talk about it, especially in the United States, where we practically worship money.

We're even more reluctant to talk about money in the context of our relationships. Money is a destabilizing factor in marriage and the nuclear weapon of choice in divorce. But it shouldn't be, and it doesn't have to be.

During my training years ago as a Certified Financial Planner™ (CFP®), I learned multiple strategies to help clients save for retirement and plan for their loved ones. But strategies to protect financial security in marriage or in case of divorce? We didn't cover the impact that divorce laws have around money, marriage and divorce, or property divisions, or how to start a conversation about money with your spouse.

Fortunately, my training as a Certified Divorce Financial Analyst® (CDFA®) covered all of the above and more. Marital law, much like business law, is where the law and money collide. People know intuitively but fail to plan for the fact that a marriage is an economic partnership like any other. Marital laws and financial realities govern the division of wealth when there is a breakup of an economic unit—the family. But when applied to your own unique situation, it's these same laws that can jeopardize your financial future. These laws cannot keep up with the evolution of the tax code, investments, or even how we earn, spend, and save money.

Have the Talk before You Take the Walk

The topic of money rarely comes up before that walk down the church aisle, garden path, or courthouse hallway. Even after the wedding, sometimes well into the marriage, the money talk stays tucked in the attic corners of couples' minds. There it sits, sometimes for decades, along with embarrassing memories from high school.

Stashing embarrassing moments away does no harm in itself, but ignoring the money talk is like having an elephant in your living room. We unconsciously tiptoe around money so as not to rock the boat. But is that what you really want your marriage to look like?

One way to start the conversation is to talk about your parents and their attitudes about money. How did they view money? Did you get an allowance? Did they help you pay for college? How did your parents save for their first home or retirement? By the time a couple starts contemplating divorce, it may be too late to have this conversation. So let go of how you think your spouse will react to it, and use the conversation to get to know your spouse better. It can strengthen the connection you already have.

Rachel and Alex

Rachel thought she wanted a divorce. She'd been married for twelve years, and her husband, Alex, ran a successful business. Rachel had been sick for a long time with a debilitating illness.

She no longer understood the money they had or whether there was enough in savings for their children's future education or her own retirement. Her racing thoughts metastasized into arguments over the smallest of things that had nothing to do with money. Alex, meanwhile, retreated to his office to avoid conflict. This validated Rachel's belief that Alex no longer cared for his family. During one of their heated debates, Rachel revealed her true fears. She was worried there wasn't enough money. But instead of running to an attorney, Alex called a close family friend who happened to be a financial planner. He showed Rachel there was plenty of money for their retirement and their children's college educations. After several meetings and some financial education, Rachel began to understand her family's resources, which calmed her fears and returned a degree of serenity to the relationship.

Rachel and Alex didn't need an argument that ended in divorce. They needed to understand each other and their money.

Fight or Flight: Only Helpful on the Serengeti

Emotions drive us throughout all of our relationships. They override our rational minds when a cooler head would clearly help more.

Studies show that, under stress, people tend to discount negative outcomes. For example, addicts who are stressed have a difficult time giving up their addictions because the positive "high" outweighs the negative "low." Think about it: During your engagement, it's all about the celebration—choosing a venue, picking out flowers, even budgeting for the wedding. It seems unnecessary to bring up her credit card debt or his unemployment. In divorce, venting anger and frustration feels good— much better than facing the financial impact. But in both cases it's the financial impact that lasts. And it's the financial impact that ultimately hurts you and your children, leaving them with less than they deserve emotionally and financially.

More often than not, men charge ahead when stressed; women are usually more cautious. A man might proclaim: "Just give my ex whatever she wants" just to be done. Later he regrets his emotional response. He either resigns that he'll have to live with his decision to leave the marriage with much less than he thinks he deserves or takes an expensive trip back into the courtroom in an attempt to change the agreement. Women tend to analyze each step of the process, buy books like this one, or hire outside professionals to help with decision making. But that approach can lead to costly "analysis paralysis," delaying the final outcome, wasting precious resources in the process. These are stereotypes, of course; you may be just the opposite.

Fear is normal. But the fight-or-flight response isn't helpful, unless your spouse has literally turned into a stampeding wildebeest. Talking about your money fears with your spouse, on the other hand, *is* helpful.

The Eerie, Creaking Floorboards in Your Mind

While you shouldn't let emotions control you, you also shouldn't deny your inner voice. Those hairs on the back of your neck stand up for a reason. If something doesn't sound right to you, it probably isn't. If your partner's reaction to the money conversation elicits one of these responses: "You're so dramatic (or emotional or paranoid)," "You're overreacting," or "Don't worry about it," pay attention. Such statements are more than mysterious, creaky floorboards you can't locate. They're big red flags.

You're not supposed to run away (like Rachel) or let your emotions run away with you. But you're not supposed to deny your emotions, either. Which is it? Answer: both and neither. Just don't wait and hope for the best. If you're convinced you can't share the money talk, admit your fears: Being vulnerable is one of the best way to build intimacy with your partner and help your marriage succeed, according to relationship therapists, who should know, right? So go ahead and open up. If one of you really, truly can't imagine having such a discussion, or if you and your partner are so touchy about money that you fight over the coins in the couch cushions, meet with a therapist or financial planner to get started.

Friend or Foe:
Talk to the Dog, Instead

Everyone wants to give you financial advice when you get engaged, get married, or are thinking about divorce. Hashing out your marital troubles with your sister/mother/friend feels good in the moment. But believe me, both the conversation and the advice that follows could cause more harm than good.

Therapists sometimes call these types of advisors "shadow figures" who have "shadow interests" and offer "shadow advice" for your marriage or during your divorce. These people seem to have had experiences uniquely close to yours, but there's always something you don't know about their situation, and often it's something really big.

Family and friends may use information you shared against you to bolster their own interests. Or worse, they might be forced to reveal confidential information about you in court during divorce, potentially harming your family's emotional and financial future. So, please, keep detailed conversations about your marital troubles private. When they start talking, just smile gratefully and excuse yourself. If you have to talk, enlist the services of a trained, professional therapist . . . or your trusty mutt.

Final Thoughts

You may feel embarrassed that you haven't paid proper attention to your financial life. "You're marrying him (or are married to him) and you don't know how much money/debt/savings he has?," or "Didn't you know about her credit card debt?" Your parents, family, or friends can't believe you let things go so far.

Failures, slip ups, and criticism are inevitable in life. But you are taking action now. You are learning the financial ropes to create an open and transparent relationship and a bright financial future. Sharing your thoughts with your partner, especially your thoughts on money, is the brave thing to do!

2

Crafting Sensible Pre- and Post-Marital Agreements

TO PROTECT YOUR MONEY IN YOUR relationship, we need to *separate* you from your emotions, but not *divorce* you from them. Your feelings matter. They may help guide you to make better choices for your unique situation.

Your intimidation, confusion, or anger about the money in your relationship deserve their proper weight in your decisions, but you need a money strategy. A strategy requires objective thinking, the right tactics, and compassion. Like all the other risks out there, divorce is a real possibility. Managing that risk is easier than you think, but it takes some effort. Steel yourself for a moment to learn how to protect the things you've worked hard for and the people you care about.

Pre- and post-marital agreements can have an important role to play in your relationship. If you understand what a marital agreement is, you'll have an easier time deciding whether to craft one. Marital agreements shouldn't be about how many times you'll have sex and when, or who will clean the garage each spring—these terms could even invalidate the whole agreement. They should be about protecting your mental health, your money, and your marriage, all at the same time. An agreement is your very own personal insurance plan. Without it, you increase the odds that you will lose if the unthinkable—divorce—occurs.

Suzanne

Suzanne was a thirty-nine-year-old nutritionist with a busy practice when she met a man and got engaged. Oh, the glorious lunch hours, evenings, and weekends spent planning the perfect day! They were exhausting, but exhilarating. How could she have imagined that, ten years later, she'd spend far more time, hundreds of hours, and thousands of dollars untangling financially from a husband who, as it turned out, was not actually that "into" women? How could she have known?

The moral of this story: If you plan to marry, then plan to divorce. Suzanne could have protected her money and her business, which was devastated by the divorce. For Suzie, financial planning seemed unnecessary at the time, like a slap in the face to the relationship—even though she knew that divorce was, statistically, a real possibility.

Ironically, Suzie planned for the worst when she thought about other risks. She carefully scrutinized her home inspection and increased the recommended insurance. She bought health insurance for her cocker spaniel and helped her mother purchase long-term care insurance. It's not as if she couldn't ever imagine worst-case scenarios. Like many of us, she just couldn't imagine them when she was in love.

Setting the terms of a marital agreement is difficult, so bring your strongest you to the planning process. Think of planning like exercise. Hard, yes, but do you know anyone who announces at the end of a workout: "Wow, I really wish I hadn't wasted an hour doing that!"

The Business End of Becoming a Couple

This book shows you how to negotiate the terms of a marital agreement, but first let's talk about what one is and what one is not.

A marital agreement is an agreement that can be written at any stage of a relationship. You can prepare one whether or not you plan to marry (a so-called *no-nup* or cohabitation agreement). Generally speaking, a marital agreement is a financial contract between couples before marriage (prenuptial) or during marriage (postnuptial) relating to the division of money and property in the event of divorce or separation. The agreement can also address how the couple uses money during marriage (but think retirement fund contributions, not the number of lattés allowed in a week). An attorney prepares the agreement, but the couple, sometimes with the help of a financial planner, must determine its terms. Without an agreement, the terms of marriage are dictated by the marital laws in the state where they live.

In order to know the terms to negotiate in a marital agreement, you'll want to have a good understanding of the laws in your state as they relate to marriage and divorce. Your marriage is governed by an area of the law in each state known as *family law*. Family law deals with family-related matters and domestic relations, including marriage, civil unions, and domestic partnerships. It also deals with the termination of relationships, divorce, alimony, child custody, and child support.

Family law defines whether money and property are separate or marital in order to determine how money and property is divided in case of divorce. Typically, the money or property you have before marriage or acquired by gift or inheritance during the marriage is separate. In divorce, proving separate property is often a big part of the fight. A marital agreement can nip this fight in the bud by clearly defining separate property or by redefining marital property as separate property and vice versa.

The way marital property is treated under family law may depend on whether your state is a community property state or an equitable division state. Community property laws are observed in ten states: Alaska (by agreement), Arizona, California, Idaho, Louisiana, Nevada, New Mexico, Texas, Washington, and Wisconsin. In these states, spouses are usually deemed equal owners of all income and assets earned or acquired during the marriage, even if only one spouse is employed. In addition, all property acquired during the marriage with *community* money is deemed to be owned equally by both the wife and husband, regardless of who purchased it. Even income earned on separate property may be owned by the community. Equal ownership also applies to debts. Both spouses are equally liable for debts, including unpaid balances on credit cards, home mortgages, and car loan balances incurred during the marriage. In community property states, child support and alimony may be formulaic and limited unless spouses can agree to other alternatives.

In equitable distribution states, property acquired during the marriage may be seen very differently by divorce courts. Divorce laws vary state by state, making it nearly impossible to predict exactly what a judge sitting in a given state would deem a "fair and equitable" property division. For example, the court may contemplate earnings potential or the value of one spouse staying at home to raise children. One spouse may receive a disproportionate amount of property based on these factors.

A pre- or post-marital agreement may eliminate much of the uncertainty about how property or income is divided in either type of state. In addition, it may provide some protection for your assets if your future spouse is involved in a lawsuit (depending, of course, on your state's law and the business structure).

Jennifer

Jennifer called her financial planner to discuss financing a future expansion of her business. During the meeting she excitedly talked about her recent marriage to a builder. She was concerned, though, about the impact his business liabilities or a divorce might have on her financial plans. Along with an attorney, her financial planner helped her prepare a post-marital agreement stating that each business was nonmarital property. The agreement also stated that Jennifer and her business would be responsible for any new debt used to finance business operations.

Happy ending here: no nagging insecurities interfering with Jennifer's marital bliss.

Preparing a pre- or post-marital agreement is the perfect opportunity for you to commit, from the very start, to an open and honest relationship. However, it generally does not address how you will ultimately support your children. The laws in your state are there in large part to protect children. Child support decisions are based on the emotional and financial state of you, your spouse, your family, and your relationship at the time of divorce, which is unpredictable until you decide to divorce. Your attorney can help you understand the line between financial agreements and legal child support.

Remember, if you don't prepare a marital agreement, your state government steps in to prepare one for you—using family law. And family law is debated by divorce lawyers in the courtroom, costing you time, money, and heartache.

Bill and Jane

In 2004, Bill bought a vacation home in Oregon. He told his wife, Jane, that it was a surprise tenth anniversary present for her. Five years later they faced divorce. Bill told his lawyer the house in Oregon was an investment and that he bought the house with his separate property. Jane told her lawyer the house had been a gift to her. A costly fight ensued.

Take the time, and have the courage to talk about "mine, yours, and ours" before marriage, or at least before your tenth anniversary! If you don't, lawyers will argue (costly) and a judge may be asked to decide (scary). Judges may not be sympathetic to your argument; they might be biased from personal experiences. After all, judges are people too, and they mess up their marriages just like the rest of us. Even more important: Judges have little time to understand your point of view.

If the example above makes you nervous—good. It should! Know the law and keep simple documentation. You'll save everyone heartache, confusion, and cash.

Now take it a step further: What if Jane had asked Bill to sign an agreement to confirm that the house was a gift five years ago? At the time, Jane didn't want to seem ungrateful, but now she wishes she could go back in time. If only she had spoken up . . . Speak up! Confirming ownership would have saved this couple thousands of dollars and a ton of headaches.

If nonmarital money is used to purchase assets owned or used by both of you, sign a letter upon purchase indicating whose nonmarital money made the purchase and whether it's a gift. Or better yet, sign a legal agreement regarding the *character* of the property (separate or marital). Keep all documentation filed along with marital agreements or other important documents such as wills.

What a Marital Agreement Isn't

There are a number of misconceptions about prenuptial and other marital agreements. Some people think a prenuptial agreement is a contract about how many dates you'll have per month or which spouse will delegate the household duties. Both are false, almost always. Most pre- and post-marital agreements cover only financial and guardianship issues. If the agreement has extreme terms, a judge may throw the whole thing out!

Even attorneys have misconceptions. Some will not draft marital agreements because they believe they are difficult to sustain in court, especially if one of the spouses, during divorce, claims to have signed under duress (in order to get married). I think this is ridiculous. It's like saying you won't prepare a will because someone might challenge it.

And speaking of wills, a marital agreement is also not a will. A marital agreement covers what happens if you decide to divorce, and you may never divorce. A will addresses what happens to your money and property should you die. It can and should have different terms. More on that at the end of this chapter.

Not Just a Pretty Face

A marital agreement is more than a token effort at openness or a way to placate a nervous lover. It is, in fact, a contract, and preparing a contract requires work. Financial data gathered from bank and investment account statements, tax returns, and the like forms the basis for your marital agreement. It can be as simple as this: an agreed to list of each spouse's accounts and property before marriage.

When one spouse owns the vast majority of separate property, or if family financial assets are complicated (and especially when assets are held in trusts), couples should consult with their own financial planners and attorneys about possible consequences of their agreement.

Marital agreements, like any legal contract, require an exchange in order to be valid. Money (or future monetary commitments) might be exchanged for giving up or limiting your rights. For example, a spouse may agree to pay a specific amount of support in case of divorce. This term is exchanged for limited rights to sue for additional support. If the agreement seems one-sided, it may not hold up in court.

It's Your Choice: Paradise or Pair of Dice?

A marital agreement can, and should, go further than simply listing the money and property you had before you wed. Many marital agreements contain additional provisions because in some states, income from separate property or property owned before marriage is a financial resource to fight over during divorce. Disagreements over who owns what just add fuel to the fire of a highly contested and expensive divorce. If you decide to divorce, a marital agreement puts you and your spouse in control of financial decisions that impact your long-term financial future, not the state or a judge.

Depending on state law, a pre- or post-marital agreement can define each source of future income from earnings or investments as separate or marital. And it can specifically state how much money or property will transfer from one spouse to another in case of divorce, which can depend on the length of the marriage.

A pre- or post-marital agreement can address things like: Will one of you support the other while one of you attends college? Whose income will pay for expenses related to property owned before marriage? It may also address the forfeiture of assets due to adultery and conditions of guardianship.

Last, a marital agreement is flexible. You must modify or amend it as your assets and your relationship change over time.

Mark and Laura

Mark and Laura both worked, and Laura, in particular, loved her job. They decided to have children and keep working. Then, Mark got a substantial inheritance, transferred into Mark's individual account under the management of his parent's financial advisor. (Oh, if we were all so lucky, right?) Mark and

Laura discussed the inheritance and decided to keep it invested. Because they felt better about their retirement and their ability to pay for college, they agreed that Mark should stay home with the children while Laura, now a corporate executive, continued to work. The arrangement seemed perfect. Both agreed that Laura would forego most of her planned 401(k) retirement contributions and use nearly all her earnings to support the family, allowing the inheritance to grow, untouched. Five years before their planned retirement, Mark and Laura divorced.

Very sad ending: The inheritance was awarded to Mark, while Laura was left with virtually no retirement savings. Laura will have to work well beyond her planned retirement date.

Laura rolled the dice and lost. She could have avoided the bad roll. Instead of their undocumented agreement to use the inheritance for retirement and college spending, Mark and Laura could have signed a post-marital agreement indicating that some or all of the inheritance was marital property. Or, if Mark balked at that, Laura might have decided to reduce expenses, increase savings, or continue making contributions to her own retirement plan.

So if your gut reaction is: "My spouse would never agree to this," please ignore your gut this time and heed your head. This is your financial life and your retirement. Talk with your spouse openly and often about your family's financial future. If you can't find the words, talk to a financial planner or a therapist for help starting the discussion.

You Gotta Spend to Save

A pre- or post-marital agreement typically costs about as much as most estate plans and wills—between $1,200 and $3,000—while a financial plan costs between $1,200 and $5,000, depending on the complexity of the couples' money and property. The ideas generated by these agreements and plans may offset much of their cost. By comparison, a divorce can run upward of $25,000. So agreement about money is cost-effective.

Another critical consideration: The high cost of divorce is not only financial, but also emotional. When financial issues are decided before or during marriage, divorcing couples can focus time and energy on healing themselves and their family.

Marital Agreements in Practice

Creating a marital agreement is step one. Understanding how to manage your money and property under the agreement is step two. Money that is commingled may no longer be separate, even if a bank or investment account was owned before marriage or inherited.

Separate property can easily become marital property that is subject to division in divorce—unless it's clearly distinguished. Depositing a gift, inheritance, or money from an account you own before marriage into a joint account may cause commingling of separate property and change the character from separate to marital property, even if the funds are not used for joint living expenses.

Sam

Sam and his wife, happily married for over ten years, had a beautiful home and a large joint investment account—worth nearly $1 million. Sam's father died, leaving him an investment account worth $50,000. Sam wanted to use the $50,000 to pay off the remaining mortgage on their home. Sam's financial planner, Joan, advised Sam that his inheritance is separate property. If he used it to pay off a jointly owned asset (like the home), he might only get half the value back if he ever divorced. Sam appreciated the advice and decided to deposit the inheritance in a separate account and use money from the joint account to pay off the mortgage.

Sam wasn't even contemplating a divorce, but his financial planner knew that divorce could happen to anyone. A separate account was the right move for him. Alternatively, Sam could have struck an agreement with his wife clearly stating that the mortgage payoff would be reimbursed to him as his separate property when the property sold and/or in case of divorce.

As a rule, couples should consider keeping nonmarital property separate from marital property. Couples should avoid using separate accounts to pay for joint purchases unless they consider the purchase as joint (meaning they will divide it in case of divorce) or they document how separate money and property are used for purchases. As for other expenses, consider contributing separate funds purposely and periodically into joint accounts for regular family expenses.

Commingling can result in a bad outcome, but it isn't always a bad thing. In fact it can be a useful and cost-effective tool to change the character of assets from separate to marital. In the earlier story about Mark and Laura, Mark could have moved some of his inheritance to their joint account over time to protect Laura and her retirement if they divorced.

Even the Best-Laid Plans Can Crumble

Another reason attorneys shy away from drafting marital agreements is that they often see marital agreements that cause more problems than they resolve. Why? Because the couple failed to update their agreement. Old investments morph into new ones, jobs change, health issues crop up—all of which makes it difficult to apply the old agreement to new realities.

Marital plans need continuous evaluation, or their terms could come back to haunt you. In case of divorce, sticking to the plan's terms and documenting changes will save not only the day but also your money.

Mary Lou and Fredrick

Mary Lou and Fredrick lived frugally, and they were happy. They married late in life and decided to strike a written agreement. Without sharing the magnitude or content of their existing investments, they agreed that their property and investments, as well as their income and earnings, before marriage and in marriage would stay separate. Mary Lou sold her small condo in a quaint little neighborhood she loved and used the money as down payment for a larger home Fredrick wanted in the suburbs. Unfortunately, Fredrick lost his job just after they married and the couple's income never fully recovered. Instead of contributing to her savings, Mary Lou covered the payments and living expenses Fredrick couldn't. Eight years later Mary Lou became ill and had to slow down at work, moving to a part-time position. All the stress led to divorce. Mary Lou asked her attorney: "Now it's Fredrick's turn. Won't I get alimony?"

The answer in this case was: "No." Plus, Fredrick kept 100 percent of his contributions to his 401(k) and the significant income from premarriage investment and retirement plans.

So plan to review and update your agreements with your financial planner and attorney periodically and especially when life changes. Mary Lou could have "loaned" Fredrick the costs she covered for him or changed their marital agreement to reflect new realities of their marriage well before divorce.

Final Thoughts

Legal agreements protect you from the unintended consequences of informal or implied agreements. All agreements should be amended as your money and relationship changes.

Action Items

❑ Educate yourself about the marital laws in your state.

❑ Prepare a list of all your financial accounts and property—
and the value of each—before you marry.

❑ Discuss the role of a marital agreement in your relationship.

❑ Update your agreement at least every three years or as your
life changes—whether it's a windfall of money or job loss.
As the money in your relationship changes, the agreement
should change, too.

3

21 Essential Documents

COLLECT THE DOCUMENTS LISTED IN THIS chapter because you and your partner *deserve to know* where your money is and how it is used. You share a bed, at least most of the time, and perhaps even a toothbrush, if one of you forgets to pack one. So please share the money talk, and review the documents together. This applies to those of you not yet married, too.

The 21 Essential Financial Documents

These are the documents that you and your partner should share and review at least annually.

1. Pay Stubs/Payroll Statements

2. Investment and Trust Account Statements

3. Tax Returns (personal, trust, and business)

4. W-2 Annual Income Statements

5. Retirement Account Statements
   (401(k)/403(b), IRA, Roth IRA, Profit Sharing)

6. Stock Option/Restricted Stock Grant Statements

7. Pension Account Statements

8. Business Ownership and Financial Statements

9. Real Estate Closing Documents

10. Real Estate Appraisals

11. Mortgage Statements

12. Health Insurance

13. Life, Disability, and Long-Term Care Insurance

14. Property and Casualty Insurance
    (Home, Auto, Umbrella, Riders)

15. Company Benefit Plans

16. Credit Card Statements

17. Auto and Boat Loans

18. Margin Debt Statements, 401(k) Loans
    against Investment, or Retirement Accounts

19. Personal, Student, and Business Loans

20. List of Other Valuable Property like Art, Coins, or Jewelry

21. Credit Reports

Gather, Gather, Gather

Now it's time to channel your inner squirrel. Round up pay stubs or payroll statements, tax returns, and investment account and bank statements. Set aside time with your spouse to review these statements and your credit reports together.

Start with payroll statements or pay stubs and your annual W-2. These show earnings from work and retirement plan contributions, as well as income from any stock options. These statements also reveal withholding for taxes, spending for health insurance in your benefit plan, and the like. The W-2 annual income summary provided at year-end by your employer shows annual income and contributions to help prepare taxes.

Next, find your tax returns. Tax returns not only show salary income but also other critically important income sources like investment interest and dividends, gift and/or trust income, business income, and rental income. Please recognize that tax returns are not evidence of all financial accounts. There may be *other assets*—property, certain retirement accounts, some checking accounts, or annuities—that neither produced taxable income nor received a contribution during the tax year. And because of the way debts and expenses are reported, tax returns may not tell you enough about mortgages, property taxes, car loans, home equity loans, or credit card debt. If you think there is more to gather, there may be more. Credit reports reveal hidden or previously unnamed financial resources and debts. Review your reports at www.annualcreditreport.com.

What about other assets and debt? Find your bank and

investment statements. These will include not only interest and dividends from savings and investment accounts reported on the tax return, but also nontaxable (unrealized) gains and total account values. The *transaction history* section of a bank or investment account statement shows deposits or withdrawals as well as investments bought and sold. Each withdrawal could help you identify income, assets, or undisclosed expenses since every withdrawal is either deposited into another bank or investment account or taken out in cash.

A financial planner can help you understand the statements you've gathered. He or she can work with you to generate a list of your accounts, property, and debts before marriage. Because everything owned or borrowed is typically separate before marriage, a couple can use this list as an exhibit showing separate property before marriage in a marital agreement. Without this list, a forensic accountant may need to work with an attorney during divorce to go back in time to find these accounts and their value before marriage. This is a costly and time-consuming process. The cost of finding or *tracing* these values after a long marriage will quickly exceed the cost of preparing a marital agreement.

Of course, if cash is hidden in the guest room mattress, no document will tell you that, and a financial planner won't find it, either. If you're already married and you suspect that money is squirreled away, you'll have to hire a private investigator.

Gail and Rob

Gail had a small investment account before marriage, and then she gained a husband, Rob, who loved to spend. From power tools to hot stone massages, spending money made Gail's husband feel good. Gail, who certainly understood the lure of a hot stone massage and also the value of her husband's self-esteem to the relationship, thought she'd keep some money for herself. She secretly contributed part of her salary to her investment account after getting married, just in case the marriage fell apart. When she divorced him, she learned that all her deposits were marital property, available for division in case of divorce.

Gail's intent was to keep her savings separate. But her good intentions were good for nothing. Because Gail didn't know how the law would treat her savings, she left the marriage with much less than she'd expected. She could have addressed her desire to have her own savings account with her husband and legally documented her intent in a pre- or post-marital agreement.

First Tackle Your Biggest Financial Nut (No, Not Your Partner; Play Nice.)

As you review documents, keep in mind what will be important in case of divorce. How and when was the bank account, property, or debt acquired? Plan to create and keep a timeline of the deposits and withdrawals associated with each major purchase during the marriage.

The largest asset (the biggest nut) acquired before or after marriage is often a home. The value you own is the appraised value less the balance owed on the mortgage. If the home is sold, the value is reduced further by selling costs (mainly repairs and payments to the realtor needed to sell the home) and taxes on the difference between the net sales price and the purchase price, less any available tax exemptions associated with the sale of the couple's primary residence.

A marital agreement can define who contributed to the down payment and address what happens to the home if the marriage ends. The couple can agree that the home will be sold or co-owned. The agreement may also address who will continue to use the home. Finally, the agreement must be amended if the couple sells the home in favor of new digs.

Jean and Scott

Jean and Scott planned to marry. Jean owned a home on the north side of town. But Scott planned to work farther south. So Jean sold her home just before they married. Two months after the wedding they moved into their new home. Jean deposited the money from the sale of her former home into their joint account and then used the full amount to pay the down payment and each mortgage payment until Scott finally got a job. Years later, when Jean and Scott divorced, Jean had to divide the home equally with Scott even though she paid 100 percent of the down payment and much more than half of all their mortgage payments.

Jean made two mistakes. First, she wasn't aware of the marital laws in her state. By adding her separate money to the joint account, she unwittingly commingled it, making it marital property. Second, she failed to get a marital agreement. She thought she was protecting Scott's self-esteem. After all, he was struggling to find the right job. There was never a good time to bring up the subject.

Other big financial "nuts" in marriage include businesses, investments, and retirement accounts. This can get tricky. An investment or business's value is typically not the value stated on an account statement. It's often less because the sale (or withdrawal) can trigger taxes or penalties.

Smaller nuts include jewelry, rugs, artwork, or coins that may need to be appraised in order to determine value. If needed, your financial planner or attorney can help you find a qualified appraisal company in your area. And take pictures since you never know when one of these items might disappear. Gold coins in the safe? You know, the ones you and your spouse won on that wild trip to Vegas? One day there are gold coins in the safe, the next day they're gone. And on the third day your spouse announces, "I want a divorce."

How Much Do You Owe?

You should also gather documents that show what you both owe: credit card statements, mortgage statements, auto/boat/personal loans, margin debt or investment/retirement account loans, student loans, business loans, and loans you may have guaranteed for someone else.

Each form of indebtedness is unique. Even if your spouse is listed as the sole owner of the debt, you may still be responsible for it. Be open and honest about your financial lives, even if your credit card is maxed out. Remember: Being vulnerable builds intimacy, which helps your marriage succeed! Hiding your vulnerabilities will only make things much more difficult in the long run.

A pre- or post-marital agreement can require how certain debts will be paid and by whom. Without agreement, a divorce court could divide the debt between both spouses. Debt acquired during marriage is typically joint debt unless a marital agreement makes one spouse responsible for it in case of divorce. Lenders, however, are only interested in getting paid, so they will probably not consider your marital agreement. More likely, they'll ignore it.

Ann and Dean

Ann and her husband, Dean, used the money from a home equity loan to buy their vacation home. The family home col-lateralized the home equity loan, meaning that if the home equity loan was not paid on time, the bank could sell the family home and use the proceeds to pay off the home equity loan. Ann and Dean divorced, leaving Ann the vacation home. Dean was awarded the family home and responsibility for the home equity loan. However, Ann was still also responsible for the home equity loan, as far as the bank was concerned. Ann was concerned that Dean might not make payments and her credit would be ruined. But her attorney had an idea (a really good one). Under the settlement agreement, Dean was required to refinance the home equity loan within one year, and Ann would be able to view statements showing that Dean continued to make payments until he refinanced. If he did not refinance or if he missed any payments, Ann was given the right to sell the family home to pay off the loan. Paying off the loan or refinancing it were the two ways Ann could remove her name from the loan, as far as the bank was concerned.

Home equity and other kinds of loans are hard to find on account statements if you don't know what you are looking for. A credit report or title search on the home is needed to find loans secured by the home, like mortgages, home equity loans, or lines of credit. Investment accounts may have debt called *margin loans* or *pledged asset lines*, which are loans against the value of the stocks and bonds in the investment account. Company retirement accounts such as 401(k)s can have debt against the investments in the retirement account called 401(k) loans. You may need a financial professional to ferret these out.

Have You Protected Your Ass(ets)?

Gather all insurance information: health insurance policies, life insurance policies, and property and casualty insurance policies, like home insurance, auto insurance, excess liability policies (umbrella policies), and insurance riders, as well as company and executive benefit policy statements.

Without insurance, assets can quickly disappear. A health scare can deplete savings and investment accounts; a fire can destroy a home. Be prepared to share documents that show how each of your assets is insured. You need to know that insurance is paid up-to-date so that each asset is protected. Before and during marriage, spouses should monitor life insurance and other beneficiary changes in consultation with their financial planner and attorney.

Have You Protected Yourself?

Taking steps to protect yourself in case of divorce doesn't mean that you'll actually get divorced, just like buying homeowner's insurance doesn't set fire to your house. Before and during marriage, there are two critical financial resources for each of you to have in your own names—a bank account, with six months' worth of money (in case your spouse ever decides to leave with everything in your joint account) and a credit card. A credit card identifying you as an "Authorized Signatory (or User)" is not good enough because your spouse (the card owner) could cut you off. A credit card account must be in your own name to count toward building your credit.

Your credit score is critical. Your credit score will determine everything from how much you pay for a loan to whether or not you can get a new apartment or job. So use the card responsibly and pay at least the minimums in a timely manner. Ideally use no more than 30 percent of the total credit you have available in order to keep your credit score sound.

If each of you has an individual investment account or retirement account before marriage, you'll probably want to start and contribute to new accounts. If you continue to invest in the pre-marriage accounts with postmarriage money, it will be difficult and costly to determine what part of the account is separate property in case of divorce. Start a new account instead.

Depending on the laws in your state, the income from separate accounts (dividends and interest earned on investments) may be considered marital property. Spouses who are aware of this rule sometimes contribute income earned on their separate accounts to a joint account after marriage, creating a joint account that can be divided in case of divorce. If this is unappealing to you both, one solution is to define any premarriage investment or retirement account as nonmarital, with growth, income, and dividends kept separately under your marital agreement.

It may not be possible to keep company retirement accounts, like 401(k)s, separate after marriage or to start a new one. If a spouse has a job with a 401(k) retirement plan before marriage (separate property), he or she will likely continue to contribute income to the same account after marriage. Because your income contributions are typically made from marital property (your income often becomes marital income once you marry), dividing this kind of account in divorce can be complicated. To save the cost of a forensic accountant in case of divorce, keep a record of account contributions, income, and annual growth during marriage throughout the life of any premarriage 401(k) accounts. When you leave your company, you may decide to move these savings to an IRA. Keep the money in a separate IRA instead of contributing it to an existing, premarriage IRA.

Divorce is not the only marital dissolution that impacts property owned by a couple. The death of one spouse can tie up marital property until it is transferred by a probate court, depending upon state laws, how the property is titled or *designated* and who is named as the beneficiary. For example, a retirement account generally passes to the beneficiary and not through the will. An estate planning attorney can help you sort through your options to protect the money you need if one of you passes.

Final Thoughts

Early in a marriage, many couples divide responsibilities—one spouse organizes family activities and the other manages the money. If this is you—STOP. Both spouses must know where family money is spent and saved.

Action Items

❏ Gather your financial documents, including all bank and investment statements, retirement account statements, employee benefit plans, pension plans, mortgage statements, other loan statements (such as auto, etc.), tax returns, insurance statements, and credit reports.

❏ Take pictures of valuable property like coins, artwork, rugs, jewelry, etc.

❏ Know when each financial account or property was acquired, how much you paid for it, and what it was worth at the time of marriage. During the marriage, track how and when you make major purchases.

❏ Determine if any of your money or property will not be considered part of the marital estate because it was acquired before marriage or by inheritance/gift.

❏ Keep your premarriage savings and investments in separate accounts. Open and contribute to new savings accounts that are either separate under your marital agreement or joint.

4

The Marital Budget

SO YOU DISCOVERED YOUR FIANCÉ OR your spouse can't seem
to load the dishwasher properly. He discovered that you always
take the biggest cookie. The honeymoon is over, but you've
both learned you can live with each other's quirks. You've also
reviewed each other's financial resources and credit and have
come to terms with those items. Next, you should plan how you
will spend and save your combined income and monitor your
agreements and credit.

Spouses need to agree on the various financial and legal
steps they will take now and renegotiate later: (1) how much
money to contribute to joint savings, emergency funds, company retirement plans, and IRAs, in addition to how they plan
to invest and protect their money; (2) whether they will create a
prenuptial agreement and, if they will, how they'll negotiate the
terms of that agreement; and (3) how to negotiate a will. If one
spouse has fallen behind on understanding family money and

investments, hire a financial planner to get both of you thinking about your financial picture and goals.

The Marital Budget

The first question nearly every engaged or recently married couple asks is: "Should we open a joint bank account?" The simple answer is: "Yes, you should." But think about maintaining your own separate bank accounts as well.

For a financial planner like me, the joint vs. individual account question is not the place to start. You first need to identify all your expenses—rent, mortgage payments, Internet access, cable TV, electricity, groceries, and the like. I've set up a detailed budget worksheet on my website. Enter all your income and expenses, and then compare your estimates to your bank and credit card statements (all of them!).

John and Mila

John worked as a commercial real estate analyst and Mila was an accountant for a large corporation. While both had good salaries and were financially independent before marriage, John earned twice as much as Mila. John and Mila planned to rent while they saved for a down payment on a new home. They both had new cars, and both made car payments. Here's what they decided to do: John and Mila contributed two-to-one to a

joint account for joint expenses but continued to pay for indi-
vidual expenses on their own. They agreed that rent, rental
insurance, car insurance, electricity, Internet/cable TV, gro-
ceries, and pet expenses were joint expenses. Those expenses
totaled $2,400 a month. John contributed $1,600 a month while
Mila contributed $800 a month from their individual bank
accounts. If, by the end of the month, joint expenses exceeded
$2,400, John and Mila would decide whether to cut back their
joint expenses or contribute more to the joint account. Both
John and Mila paid for individual expenses like haircuts,
clothing, auto payments, student loans, and the like from their
own individual accounts, and both contributed to their retire-
ment plans at work.

And to top it off, John and Mila also opened two joint savings accounts: One to provide a year of expenses for emergencies
and a second to begin to save for their very own home! Now
that's a great start, but remember to review a plan like this as
income and expenses change.

Negotiating the "Stay-at-Home" Budget

What happens when one parent decides to stay home to care for
children? Or when a spouse takes a volunteer position because
one income is enough for both?

The longer a stay-at-home spouse stays out of the workforce, the longer it takes to get back into it. In case of divorce, the working parent gains additional work experience and typically will expect to have a more successful career trajectory and post-divorce financial life. So while one continues to climb that ladder, the other is stumbling around the tool shed looking for it.

Do not assume that *alimony* (spousal support) is automatic for a stay-at-home spouse. In some states it's nearly impossible to get anything other than already-limited child support. In other states, legislatures are faced with increasing pressure to limit support. This is especially true when the stay-at-home parent has a college education or previous work experience.

If a nonworking parent expects to leave the relationship with enough money to survive until he or she can return to the workforce, the couple needs to discuss how that will happen. Before it happens. Even though it won't happen. *(But it could.)*

Each situation is unique and, as I've said before, a financial planner can help sort out your options and an attorney can draft your agreement. One way for the stay-at-home spouse to plan for the risk of divorce is a pre- or post-marital agreement that requires a specific monthly spousal support payment or single lump sum payment that could increase with each marital anniversary. Remember that the stay-at-home spouse will need at least nine to twelve months of income for support before returning to the workforce—and additional funds if the parent stayed home for more than five years or if she (and it's still more commonly a she) is close to retirement age.

Without a formal agreement, couples will need to save so there is enough cash to divide and support the stay-at-home spouse as he or she ventures back into the workforce. If one parent will stay home, keep room in the marital budget to save at least one year of salary for every three to five years of marriage in addition to the couple's six to twelve months of emergency savings. This way, there is more money to divide in case of divorce.

The ugly truth is that most couples don't save or plan for the risk of divorce. Instead, they live beyond their means and gamble their financial lives only to find out that the credit cards are maxed out, the house has little equity, and nothing's left in the bank account when the relationship ends. Houses (and sometimes cars or other property) must be sold fast at a fire-sale price so the stay-at-home parent can afford to make it until he or she can get the additional education or training required for reentry into the workforce. Although it's unfair, time and time again I see the working spouse continue to earn as before while the stay-at-home spouse struggles to get even close to the couple's previous standard of living.

Till Debt Do Us Part

Another question that often comes from newlyweds: "Should we get a joint credit card?" The answer: "Probably not."

Having and using a credit card appropriately builds credit and helps you reduce future borrowing costs and insurance rates. Good credit may even help you land a coveted job, because potential employers may look at your credit report.

The rating agencies like Equifax and TransUnion want you to have credit, but they don't want you to use all of it. They will look at the ratio of borrowing (credit card usage) to total credit available. If it's below 30 percent and you pay your minimums on time, your rating will likely stay higher.

In a community property state like Texas, spouses are responsible for each other's debt whether it's on a joint card or not. However, courts may consider excessive spending by one spouse, or spending on a new boyfriend or girlfriend, and allocate accordingly.

Stella and Ira

Stella and Ira got married and got a joint credit card. Ira took care of the bills. They filed for divorce five years later. It turns out that Ira used the card to help support his gambling habit and girlfriend. He missed several payments, and Stella had to hire an investigator to find him. The card company came after Stella for payment. Her credit score was ruined. She was turned down for a car loan even though she had the income to pay for it.

The possible benefits of a joint card—the ability to see what your spouse buys and having some control over payment—do not compensate for the downside, which is this: The credit card company will want 100 percent of the payment from you if your spouse refuses to pay. Establish credit on your own and use it responsibly.

Insurance:
An Extra Blanket at the End of the Bed

Newly married couples must review their insurance needs. Let's look at the most common types of insurance.

HEALTH INSURANCE

Health insurance protects your financial stability. Without it, your savings could dwindle away. Both of you need at least a minimum level of protection provided by your employer or under the Affordable Health Care Act (ACA, otherwise known as ObamaCare). If coverage at work is not an option, check with a local insurance agency to review your options and see if your income qualifies you for subsidies under ACA. If you already receive a subsidy, your combined marital income may disqualify you. You will need to budget for this extra expense.

PROPERTY AND CASUALTY INSURANCE

Property and casualty insurance includes insurance on your cars, homes, and property. Your agent can help you understand the changes needed. Let the agent know where you plan to live and when you'll marry.

Combining auto insurance will save money *unless* one spouse has a poor driving record. If you or your spouse has a poor driving record or credit, ask your agent if you can get a better deal by maintaining separate policies. Adding an umbrella policy (personal liability coverage) is an inexpensive way to protect your money from excessive lawsuits.

LIFE INSURANCE

If you are newly married and have no children, purchase at least enough life insurance to cover joint debt like mortgages. If you have children, you may want to get enough life insurance to cover their needs until age twenty-five or more. How much insurance depends on your income and a concept called *human life value*. An agent can help you decide how much coverage you need.

Consider getting a policy that doesn't depend on employment with any one company because when you leave that company there will be a gap in your coverage, and you will be older. The same insurance will likely be more expensive to replace.

A life insurance policy defines the owner, the payer, the insured, and the beneficiary of the insurance. The owner decides the beneficiary and can change the beneficiary. These decisions are particularly important for estate planning in second marriages. An insurance agent or financial planner can help you decide who will play what role best for each policy.

Finally a note of caution: There are many types of life insurance. Term life insurance is *pure insurance*. You pay a premium, and the insurance company pays your beneficiaries only if you die. There are other types of life insurance, and each can have a role to play to protect your money. Some are sold as a way to protect money from lawsuits or as a tax-deferred way to save for retirement. Premiums may be much higher. As an investor in these policies, you may be able to defer taxes on the income, dividends, or capital gains generated by your contribution until you withdraw the money in retirement. But these benefits come with a cost, and there could be a catch. A qualified insurance agent or financial planner can help you navigate your options. Discuss your needs with more than one agent or planner, compare costs, and ask about commissions and fees.

DISABILITY AND LONG-TERM CARE INSURANCE

Did you know that you are more likely to become disabled than die before age 65? Your emergency savings account will cover a short-term disability but probably can't handle a long-term condition. You may want to consider disability insurance.

You may already have disability insurance at work, but do you understand how the payment is calculated or whether it depends on if you can do your specific job or any job? Is the 60 percent of base salary offered in many plans enough, or do you depend on commissions and bonuses? What if you leave the company just before you become disabled? You may want more insurance than your company provides, and like life insurance, you may not want to depend on your current employment to be covered for disability. If so, consider adding a policy outside work that covers your basic expenses.

Another type of protection to consider is long-term care insurance, particularly for those age fifty or older. People are living longer but not necessarily better. Long-term care insurance provides coverage if you or your spouse ever needs in-home or other assistance when you lose the ability to do two of the activities of daily living (ADLs)—which include bathing, toileting, dressing, feeding yourself, walking, and getting in and out of a bed or chair by yourself—or have serious cognitive disabilities like dementia or Alzheimer's.

Disability and long-term care insurance protect the healthier spouse just as much as the one needing care, but they are expensive. One way to reduce the premium expense may be to extend what's called the *elimination period*. This is the period of time between the onset of the disability and benefit payments. The longer the elimination period, the lower the premium. Again, a qualified insurance agent or financial planner can help you navigate your options. Discuss your needs with more than one agent or planner, compare costs, and ask about commissions and fees.

ESTATE PLANS:
YOUR MARITAL BED'S HEIRLOOM QUILT

How long have you known your spouse? A year, maybe two? Do you really want to leave all (or even most) of your money and belongings to him or her? Probably not.

Preparing a will is the next logical and critical step for financially compatible couples. If you don't prepare a will and estate plan, your state government does that for you (just like your marriage agreement); it's called *Intestate Succession Law*.

Many assets pass through wills to beneficiaries in a process called probate. Still other assets pass to the beneficiary directly. Rules vary for different types of assets. For example, you may be required to list your spouse as the beneficiary of your qualified plans like 401(k)s unless he or she gives you permission to name someone else. If your children from a previous marriage will benefit from your 401(k) account instead, you and your fiancé should talk about and agree on this before you marry.

Estate planning advice is especially important when your plan includes more than just your spouse and the children you have together.

Pam and Mitch
(My Own Story)

Mitch and I married in 2014. This is my first marriage and his second. I have no children. My husband has two adult children.

We decided to live in the house I own. We have a marital agreement stating that he will not make a claim on the house if we divorce. But what if I die? My will covers that. If I get hit by a bus, I don't want my family to kick him out of the house. So in our will, after five years, the house will pass to my niece. She can live in it, sell it, or rent it to Mitch—anything she wants.

Why was the will so important? If I died without a will, the house could pass to my husband and he could pass it to his children under interstate laws. My niece, who is so important to me, would be left out.

In 2016, Mitch and I purchased a new home and in 2018 I sold my house. We memorialized these changes by amending our marital agreement and wills first in 2016 and again in 2018.

Drawing up a will is difficult. You want to care for each other, but each one of us has other people we care about, too. As with any marital agreement, use this opportunity to grow closer, to listen to a partner's needs, and to help them understand yours.

An estate planning attorney can help you prepare your will and other supporting documents, like medical and financial power of attorney documents, so a trusted someone can make decisions for you if you become incapacitated.

All marital agreements, wills, and estate plans can and should evolve as your relationship grows. You should review your plan whenever you make a significant purchase or sale of property, come into an inheritance, or at least every five years.

Final Thoughts

Financial planning early on or during a relationship is difficult, so give yourself credit for reading this. Budgeting may mean your spouse has to come clean about his spending habits or that you have to admit you have no savings. Planning marital agreements and estate plans are even more stressful since you don't know what the future may hold. Be patient—with yourself and your spouse. This is real work. Take breaks in the conversation to do something fun, but then get back to work. Consider hiring professionals to help guide you, and plan to update budgets and agreements as your life changes

The plans you make now will be the foundation of your financial security whether or not your marriage lasts "for as long as you both shall live."

Action Items:

☐ Prepare a marital budget. Decide which expenses are joint and which are separate.

☐ Establish a joint emergency fund, but also fund a bank account in your own name, and have your own credit card so that you have access to money in case of job loss, emergencies, or divorce.

☐ If one of you decides to stay home or work without pay, prepare a marital agreement that reflects your needs if you divorce. Alternatively, have sufficient funds saved to support the stay-at-home spouse while he or she restarts a career and financial life after divorce or death.

❏ Protect yourself with insurance that fits your lifestyle and budget.

❏ Prepare a will and estate plan. Most likely, it will be very different from your marital agreement.

5

Smart Couples Know the Divorce Process

WHETHER YOU THINK YOU'LL NEVER DIVORCE or you've already decided to divorce, keep reading. Anyone now married may eventually join the ranks of the other 50 percent—the 50 percent that divorces. Understanding how the divorce process works is an important part of planning for your future financial security, whether you are engaged, happily married or contemplating divorce.

In truth, the oft-quoted divorce percentage above is not an accurate one, according to current research. Still, we don't need to split hairs on top of splitting everything else. The point is: If you do decide to divorce, you will have a lot of company. The good thing about having so much company is that many professionals have developed the expertise you will need as you maneuver through a divorce. It's not a cakewalk, but it's not a marathon, either. If you're smart, it might be a friendly little 10K (without the medal, but with your pride and finances intact).

Seek Détente, Not War

When you're sure that you and your spouse are splitting, work out the major issues first without an attorney—either on your own or, ideally, with your spouse. Simply speaking, if your issues are primarily financial, get financial advice first. A Certified Divorce Financial Analyst® (CDFA®) will help you understand your financial picture. Options other than a divorce, like a post-marital agreement, might work for your unique situation. If your issues are primarily child-related, start with a parenting plan specialist or therapist.

The battle cry—"I'm calling an attorney"—puts too much emphasis on the legal aspect while ignoring the underlying goals and issues in your unique situation. When you're ready to hire attorneys, know where to look and what to find out. More on that later.

As a financial planner and analyst working with divorcing clients, I see divorcées in my office and everywhere else I go. As I explain that I help people get the most value out of the money they have during divorce, the response is always some version of the lament: "I wish I had met you before my divorce." The postdivorce crowd understands (too late) that money was a key factor in their divorces. Many sought legal advice instead of financial advice; others ignored money issues in their divorce even though they knew they'd be living on half what they did before. Money issues crept up one, two, and three years after settlement, requiring expensive trips back to court, or cash to pay unexpected bills or taxes.

Heather

Heather came to see me well after she signed her divorce decree. She and her ex had investments that included a $200,000 college plan. The plan was essentially awarded to her thirteen-year-old son, Ben, with Heather's ex as the custodian of the account. Ben was a good student and likely to get a substantial scholarship. Heather was upset because she couldn't see the statements anymore, and the decree said nothing about what might happen if her son's college savings went unused. I explained to her that the account was called a 529 Plan. Although there would be taxes and penalties, Heather's ex-husband might be able to withdraw the funds without having to divide them with her.

What happened? Heather's ex-spouse withdrew the money in the plan when he remarried two years later. Their son got a scholarship, but none of the savings was available to Heather or her other children. Her only recourse was an expensive trip back to court.

Financial professionals deal with sophisticated investments and complex tax issues every day. If Heather or her attorney had sought financial knowledge about these plans, the decree could have been more specific—requiring that unused funds get divided equally, or be allocated to the couple's other children.

Maybe Heather's ex didn't know that their other children could benefit from these savings or that dividing the unused portion was needed to "equalize" the property division. Because

Ben got a scholarship, perhaps Heather's ex thought the money was now his. After all, he was the custodian. If the decree had been clear, he might have known what to do, and both he and Heather would have avoided the expense and stress of another courtroom drama.

Crafting a final settlement agreement with an attorney, but without the advice of an experienced financial professional, is like baking a cake without eggs. And you know how that will turn out! You want an attorney who understands the complexities of your financial picture and works well with your financial analyst. Good divorce attorneys know that they are experts in the legal realm but that they cannot keep up with changes in the financial realm. Armed with the expertise of a financial analyst, these attorneys negotiate for the best possible financial outcome in divorce.

Jim and Katy

Jim stayed at home with his two children from a previous relationship while Katy spent her days traveling the world consulting on high-tech projects for a large corporation. She understood high-tech companies, so she invested in the stock of a few of them. When her career slowed down a bit and the children got older, Jim returned to work part time. Katy decided she wanted more children. Jim didn't, so they decided to split. Katy was awarded the home, and Jim was awarded Katy's investment accounts, each worth $300,000. Jim's *attorney suggested that Jim withdraw from the account in order to purchase a home for himself. Katy's high-tech investments had grown significantly but were risky. A few of the stocks fell in value just before Jim could sell the shares. There was also a large back-end fee to sell some of the investments in the account. After losses, taxes, and fees, Jim ended up with only $225,000, less than he needed to purchase the home he wanted and much less than Katy received at settlement. Meanwhile, Katy sold the home a year later for $350,000, and the gain on the home was exempt from taxes.*

You only have one chance to get this right, so take time to get the best financial analyst possible. You may already have someone who invests your money, but a financial advisor who analyzes stocks or manages portfolios of investments may not provide the appropriate options or advice for marriage or divorce. A lion tamer is trained to work with lions, not elephants. What you need is a Certified Divorce Financial Analyst, or CDFA®.

A CDFA® is specifically trained to provide financial analysis for the transition into or out of marriage. You can find CDFA®s in your area on the Institute for Divorce Financial Analysts website at www.institutedfa.com. A CDFA® with other designations, such as a Certified Financial Planner (CFP®) designation, has the expertise to craft comprehensive financial agreements that are flexible and can grow with you and your family over time. And CDFA®s are often great resources for helping you choose the remaining players on your team. Experienced CDFA®s will likely know attorneys with expertise that can make a difference in your case. They also will know marriage and family therapists who can help you find the best way to express financial fears and doubts.

Engaging help from a CDFA® doesn't mean you'll get divorced. Instead it will help you understand the resources of your family and the potential financial outcomes of a divorce. Like Rachel and Alex in chapter one, you may decide to stay married or pursue some type of legal separation—or even negotiate a separation of financial assets under a post-marital agreement.

Steven

Steven grew up on a farm in rural Oklahoma. His family struggled to get him the education they knew he needed to start a different life. Now a technology executive at a mid-sized firm, Steven and his wife were doing well. They had significant savings and invested periodically in local start-up companies. A few of these investments soared while others soured, but Steven and his wife took pride in the social status of being local investors. They were invited to all the best parties and events. Steven's wife, by now an experienced investor and even more connected, had begun to invest their nest egg without his consent. And, he said, her spending was out of hand. Even though he still loved her and she was a good mom, he told me he wanted it to stop. He wanted control so he could have financial security—the kind of financial security his parents never had. Instead of filing for divorce, we created a postnuptial agreement regarding some of the couple's property, investments, and accounts. His wife agreed to the plan. He could invest his accounts as he saw fit and she hers.

In Steven's case, filing for divorce might have sounded the alarm and stirred the pot. Instead, their agreement took a big chunk of Steven's financial insecurity off the table without the emotional strain or drama of a divorce. Will this agreement help Steven and his wife move forward in their marriage, or will it end in divorce? I don't know. But even if they do divorce, dividing their money will be a much more manageable issue.

If divorce really is what you want, an attorney will want to see your balance sheet (list of property, investments, and debt) and budget before setting off to work on your case. You can find examples and worksheets to help you create these on my website. In particular, attorneys are interested in how your investments or accounts came into your family's holdings so they can figure out whether accounts and property are separate or marital. A CDFA® will help you prepare those documents and advise you on how to divide property in a way that considers, or possibly avoids, taxes and fees—all of which makes time with your attorney more productive and less costly.

When you enter the legal process knowing the financial resources available in the marriage, you can propose a workable financial division from the start, instead of fishing for one, all while navigating the other emotional, legal, and physical realities of divorce. The actual division is typically negotiated (or argued) by the couple, often with the help of mediators, or attorneys, not financial experts. And unless you already agree with your spouse or have a marital agreement, it's also the attorneys and the judge who will determine if any money or property (assets) might be considered separate property.

The final and perhaps the most important reason to attempt to work out issues before you see an attorney is cost. Divorce is very expensive, especially in comparison to the cost of knowledgeable financial planning. In divorce, attorneys routinely charge $350–$500 an hour or more. According to the International Association of Collaborative Professionals, the average case ranges from $17,800 (no children involved) to $25,600 (with children). Litigated divorces can cost up to three times more. You'll save real money by going into the process knowing what you have and what resources you need to move forward.

More people on your team doesn't have to mean more cost. In the long run, getting the right advice will save you time and money.

Save the Drama for the Diary

I regularly see clients who are angry and confused. They want their attorneys to help them get "their day in court." But the courtroom process is expensive, unpredictable, and often unnecessary. Most courts have backlogs of cases, so judges have little time to understand the nuances of yours. In other words: Your case is special, but it's really only special to you.

Also worth knowing: Court proceedings are a matter of public record. Unlike Vegas, what happens in divorce court does not stay in divorce court. As an analyst, I often take part in or observe cases at the courthouse. Recently, I watched a hearing to establish which spouse would stay in the home during the divorce process. The husband worked from home and kept an office there. The wife often traveled for work. She also spent weeks of her own free time as a volunteer travel guide outside the country. She'd accused her husband of an extra-marital relationship with an assistant "who'd never even been to Europe." She also blurted out that the assistant wore "sexy sweats" to work in the husband's home office. These bits were mostly irrelevant to the proceeding, of course, but the wife felt compelled to share the information.

Anyone could have walked into the courtroom and become familiar with the couple's immense loads of "dirty laundry." Divorce proceedings are public, and whatever is filed is available for anyone to read. Why didn't this couple settle in private? Were they that angry? Or just unaware that anyone could listen in?

I encourage my clients to avoid (or at least minimize) courtroom drama. Find a process and a group of professionals to help you negotiate the best outcome for your situation.

The Agreed Upon Divorce

Ideally, couples agree to broad terms together with the help of financial analysts and parenting experts before hiring attorneys. The couple's attorneys provide legal advice. Couples take it upon themselves to weigh the value of legal rights against their financial and emotional goals (and their budget). The attorneys then trade ideas and documents based on the couple's instructions until an agreement is reached–saving time, money and drama in the process. If an agreement can't be reached, the process goes to mediation around the couple's points of disagreement.

Mediation: An Alternative to Judge, Jury, and Executioner

Mediation has gained popularity in the last several years as a means of resolving disputes in divorces. Whether by choice or court-ordered mandate, the process is a negotiation between spouses, mediated by an attorney or other professional. The mediator may suggest a potential outcome, but the decision to accept or reject the proposed outcome remains with the couple. Mediation is nonbinding, meaning that the mediator cannot force any result. Arbitration is similar, but an agreement among a panel of arbitrators may be binding. Lawyers may or may not be involved in either process, but having representation keeps spouses informed of important legal rights and implications.

The legal advice you receive from your attorney during mediation is sometimes presented as a warning. For example, an attorney might tell her client that a mediated settlement offer is better than what a judge might decide based on a strict inter-pretation of the law or his or her experience in the courtroom.

Mediation offers a straightforward way to gather information and make decisions, and it typically takes less time and money than a courtroom settlement, but it should never be viewed as a shortcut to divorce. In addition to legal advice, couples will need financial, parenting, and emotional help, ideally before they mediate. Good advice at the onset increases the odds that you will come to an agreement outside the courtroom. It will also decrease the odds of fighting in court later over items you may have missed the first time.

Mediation can work, but please don't ignore your gut or your legal rights. If your spouse can't seem to start the process or you believe he or she is hiding accounts, you may want the legal pro-tection afforded by litigation. You deserve to know your rights and may need the courtroom process to exert them. The bene-fits may outweigh the financial and emotional expense of litiga-tion. For example, if you believe significant property or a large account is missing (or hidden) from the list of marital assets, you may need the litigated process to bring that asset into the discussion. It could be worth the cost.

Collaborative Divorce: Cool, Calm, and Complicated?

In recent years, more attorneys have turned to collaborative divorce as an alternative to mediation and litigation. While the title conjures pleasing images of couples working together to resolve issues, the process can be just as difficult and time consuming as a mediated or even courtroom process.

The goal of the collaborative process is similar to that of a prenuptial or other marital agreement. The couple creates and negotiates the terms together instead of having terms dictated by state law. Each partner must provide a list of interests (both financial and nonfinancial), as well as all financial documents and related information needed to make good decisions.

Typically the collaborative process includes a series of meetings with the couple, their attorneys, a neutral therapist, and a neutral financial professional. The attorneys are there to ensure that you know your rights under law. The other professionals are there to help negotiate a settlement between you and your spouse without strict adherence to the legal requirements in your state. Unlike most mediations, couples also hear the advice of *both* attorneys. This minimizes the impact if one of you has hired a "better" attorney.

If you have children, a neutral therapist provides them with a voice. A neutral therapist can also help guide the discussion to make the time spent in the process more productive by focusing on the future, not the past. The neutral financial professional in a collaborative divorce provides unbiased financial advice on how to preserve money, minimize taxes, and divide your money and property. The process still allows both spouses to use their own non-neutral therapeutic or financial advisors whose interests are aligned with their own.

The collaborative process works best for couples who can openly and honestly talk about their needs and financial resources during divorce. The collaborative process is a great first step toward co-parenting, and it may offer greater privacy. But there are downsides to this process. Unlike a litigated (court) process, there is no *discovery*, or legal means to help identify hidden financial assets. If the collaborating couple cannot agree, the process ends and the couple must find new attorneys and other professionals to help them resolve their issues in mediation or court.

As I said above, litigation ultimately may be the right process for you. This is especially true if you feel that your spouse is hiding significant assets and your rights under the law need to be protected.

Choosing to use mediation, collaboration, or the courtroom each has its own pros and cons that depend on your unique situation. Talk to more than one attorney. Ask each what process he or she uses most often and why, and then determine whether their favorite processes fit well with your goals in divorce.

Great Questions to Ask a Divorce Attorney

Many of my clients found their attorney by referral or online. It's a good start, but be sure you get value for the price you'll pay. A low-cost attorney may cost you much more in the long run. Here's what you need to look for:

Experience: Any attorney can practice family law, but family law is a specialized field. You will likely be better served by a lawyer whose focus is on family law. Look for an attorney who is board certified in family law or is a member of the Academy of Matrimonial Lawyers.

Timeline: The attorney should educate you on everything— filing a petition, negotiating temporary orders, mediation, collaborative divorce, and going to court.

Cost: Attorneys may charge for an initial meeting. They may require an initial *retainer* or initial fee to cover the first ten to fifteen hours of work, or they may invoice hours at a fixed rate. An attorney who charges $400 per hour may ultimately cost less than one who charges $300. It depends on how many hours he or she worked and what other hours must be accounted for (paralegals, travel time, phone calls). The overall cost also depends on the level of cooperation and the degree of disagreement between you and your spouse. Agree to a rate, but set limits. Consider using a credit card (if you can qualify, a card offering at least a year at a low- or zero-percentage rate works well). You will have more cash available to you in divorce this way—and believe me you'll need that cash. Ask if you will be responsible for filing fees or using processor servers or other professionals like accountants or therapists.

Communication: Ask prospective attorneys if they use phone, email, or text to communicate. Also find out how often you should expect contact, how long they take to return calls, and whether they charge for phone calls. Find out how electronic files are secured and sent to you. Ask your attorney to introduce you to the paralegals who will work on your case.

Other Divorce Team Members

This book provides the education you need to resolve the financial burdens of your case. A Certified Divorce Financial Analyst (CDFA®) can educate you about financial matters, but other professionals can have an equally important role to play. I'm saying it one more time! Adding professionals to your divorce team can make your divorce *more* affordable.

A **real estate appraiser** will provide an appraisal of your real property, such as your home. For most residential property, a real estate agent can create a comparative market analysis (CMA). If you and your spouse agree, the CMA may be enough to determine the value of your home. If not, your attorney or divorce financial analyst can help you find a licensed appraiser who will provide a report for use in court.

Therapists and parenting experts can help you make important decisions during the divorce process and adjust to your new single life after divorce. These experts can help you and your spouse create a negotiated parenting plan, often required by the court to minimize the chance that disagreements about the children end up there. The plan covers scheduling, carpools, activities, vacations, religion, schools, medical care, and discipline. These agreements cannot possibly cover every eventuality, particularly if your children are young. You will have to negotiate many parenting issues well beyond the divorce. The parenting plan is a reference to help decide which parent or other expert makes the final decision.

When making commitments under the parenting plan

or settlement, understand that anything you agree to is now part of your divorce *contract*. In divorce, you may be legally responsible for your child's support—food, shelter, and medical care. If you agree to pay for expenses that you are not legally required to pay (e.g. cars, college), you may have inadvertently turned a moral obligation to help into a legal one. Discuss the long-term impact of these commitments with your attorney and financial professionals.

Certified public accountants (CPA®s) and forensic accountants may be called in to trace funds or investments to determine if they are *separate property* or *marital property*. Remember that in some states, separate property can all too easily become marital just by moving the money into a joint account. These advisors may also look at tax liabilities or the tax impact of various strategies to divide money and property.

CPA®s and forensic accountants tend to focus their attention on how money became part of a couple's life—in the past. While a CDFA® can assist in this process, more often a CDFA® provides an analysis of the negotiated asset division, budget, and financial projections moving forward to preserve and save money beyond the case.

A **business valuation expert** provides an appraisal of the value of a company owned by one or both spouses. The value of the business is typically based on projections of future cash flows (income less expenses). For example, consider a business that generates $100,000 of cash flow. The valuation expert will make assumptions about how fast the cash flow will grow and whether the cash flow is certain or risky in the future. These assumptions can greatly influence the value of the company, and they can be challenged. A second business valuation expert or a financial analyst may be required to rethink or debate the original assumptions.

Your share of the business and other assets will depend on when the business started or when the investment was acquired. A valuation expert may use a *coverture fraction*. For example, if you were married ten years ago and the business started fifteen years ago, two-thirds of the value is marital. Two-thirds of the value may be divided in divorce.

Your Security

While I don't want to cause any unnecessary anxiety, I would kick myself for not including a word about your own security at the onset of divorce. Change your accounts and passwords if you believe your spouse might have unwanted access to your cell phone, texts, social media accounts, separate bank accounts, or emails. If you feel personally threatened, do not hesitate to seek the assistance of an attorney or the police to get you the protection and resources you need.

Technologies like GPS and spyware are out there, so be aware. Your attorney and financial analyst can help you find professionals that search for this type of invasion of your privacy and the legal implications of any of these violations.

Final Thoughts

Let go of the desire to have your "day in court." You may think you'll come out smelling like a rose. Even if you're certain you *are* a rose, and your spouse is a rotten apple, you probably won't feel or smell like one if you approach divorce with revenge in mind.

Address complicated financial, parenting, and emotional issues first. Avoid drama in the courtroom. You will save time, money, and maybe even self-respect if you hire the right professionals from the start.

Action Items

❏ Work with professionals on the most important aspects of your case—a parenting expert if children are involved, and/or a CDFA® when money is an issue—before you see an attorney.

❏ If money is a primary issue (and I assume it is, since you are reading this book), identify Certified Divorce Financial Analysts in your area at www.insitutedfa.com and interview more than one.

❏ Interview attorneys. Choose one who has the right combination of process and cost that fits your unique situation.

❏ Ask your CDFA® and attorney for help choosing other professionals—appraisers, therapists, CPA®s, etc.

6

Support Payments

EVER HAVE A FRIEND WHOSE EYES light up whenever you mention a rough spot in your life? Someone who serves advice like it's a plate of chicken cordon bleu when you know her family eats toaster waffles for supper?

Friends and family members (usually those with a truckload of drama in their own lives) will offer advice about alimony and child support. They mean to help, of course, but their advice can actually contribute to long-term economic loss. Ask them to provide a bag of takeout Chinese or a bottle of zinfandel instead. Then listen to your attorney and your financial analyst.

Dr. and Mrs. Tinker

Dr. and Mrs. Tinker were pillars in their community's most prestigious social circle. When they decided to divorce, Mrs. Tinker insisted on receiving alimony, just like her wealthy friends. Despite advice from her attorney and financial analyst, Mrs. Tinker turned down her husband's $1.5 million diversified investment portfolio in favor of receiving $10,000 a month for ten years. After all, that's what her friends got.

Ten years later, Mrs. Tinker is a pillar in the community's poor house (well, she's a tenant in a rent-controlled high-rise). If she had listened to her attorney and financial analyst, she could have taken the portfolio and invested it wisely. If she'd received even just a 4 percent annual return, she could still have taken $10,000 a month from it and might have preserved over $700,000 to boot after ten years. And she would never have to worry whether her check would arrive in the mail each month.

Be a thinker, not a Tinker. Know your rights under the law. Analyze and compare the value of all financial options.

Alimony—A Latin Word Meaning "Food and Sustenance," Not "All the Money"

Alimony or spousal support (also known as spousal maintenance) is a court-ordered or contractual payment for a spouse who ends up with an income disadvantage. Sometimes it's part of a settlement agreement because a couple is unable to divide an asset like real estate or a business. For divorce agreements before 2019, the payment can be tax deductible for the payer and taxable to the receiving spouse. Under new tax laws, alimony awarded in divorce settlements after December 31, 2018 are not deductible to the payer nor are they taxable to the spouse who receives support. Depending on state laws and the type of alimony paid, alimony may be either enforceable (which may include garnishment of wages or jail time if left unpaid) or modifiable under certain conditions such as job loss.

In order to determine the amount of alimony, courts generally consider a person's ability to meet reasonable needs as well as the spouse's ability to pay. Factors include the length of the marriage, age, standard of living, value of assets, health, occupation, economic needs, skills (ability to earn money), and what's needed to take care of children. Alimony is not typically awarded in marriages of five years or fewer. Alimony is typical in marriages lasting more than twenty years when one of the spouses was the primary breadwinner and the other stayed home to care for children. In between these two, there are no hard and fast rules. In mediation, a couple can agree to support payments outside these rules, but only by mutual agreement.

Depending on the type of alimony and state law, alimony may be modified if a spouse loses a job, or if the recipient spouse loses income due to an accident or earns more income due to a promotion. There may be adjustments for inflation or an escalator clause where the payments increase with the paying spouse's increase in income. If the recipient remarries or dies, the alimony typically terminates.

The IRS has lots of rules regarding what is and isn't alimony. New tax laws or the IRS can change these rules, so be sure to work with professionals who understand current rules. Alimony payments must be paid in cash, and you cannot live with your spouse when you pay or receive alimony. Payments cannot include property upkeep or the use of the paying spouse's property. Alimony can include life insurance premiums (if the spouse owns the policy), mortgage payments, taxes, and insurance on a jointly owned home if the decree requires such payments.

Alimony is usually in the form of monthly payments from one spouse to the other. These payments can be court ordered or contractual. Your attorney will explain the difference to you, but generally speaking, contractual alimony is paid out like any other contract. You'll be back in court in a contract dispute if your spouse stops making payments.

Herb and Alice

Herb stopped by his ex-wife Alice's house to fix a clog in her sink. At the beginning of the following month, Alice got her support check from Herb—less $200. Herb folded this check into a note. The note said he was deducting $200 from her alimony payment because he saved her $200. She didn't have to hire a plumber.

Dear Alice: You should have hired a plumber. Whether the alimony payment was court ordered or contractual as part of your divorce agreement, you had the right to the full amount unless the contract says otherwise. Herb can't set his own rate or get "paid" for the work he did for you. And if Herb tries to deduct the full amount of alimony on his taxes, he may face penalties.

Your attorney can educate you about your rights to alimony, which vary from state to state. In Texas, for example, alimony is limited to those married more than ten years—except in the case of disability or family violence that impedes earning power. How much support a Texas court will consider is based on a number of factors, including age, employment history, and skills, as well as property brought into the marriage. Any change in circumstances can change support. By comparison, a California court has tremendous discretion to award alimony based on the standard of living established during the marriage.

Which is better—alimony or an investment account, property or other item that can be transferred upon settlement? If there is a choice and the value is the same, I think most people prefer to have the money today (bird in the hand) instead of taking smaller payments over time. This is where financial analysis really comes in handy. Using present value calculations, a CDFA® can help you compare today's value of proposed alimony with the value of a bank account, investment account, or property. Think back to Mrs. Tinker. Her alimony was worth only about $1 million in today's dollars, one-third less than the $1.5 million dollar account offered to her.

Alimony can also be exchanged for other financial benefits. Up until 2017, a stay-at-home (or low-wage) wife might trade the right to tax exemptions for a dependent child to her highly compensated husband in exchange for more alimony or alimony over a longer period of time. Under new tax laws, all personal exemptions, including those for dependent children, are suspended from December 31, 2017 until December 31, 2025. Instead the standard deduction is increased for single, head-of-household and married filers. However, parents can negotiate who will claim the Child Tax Credit. A CDFA® or CPA can help assess which financial benefits are still available and whether the value is worth a trade-off.

Child Support:
Who Will Pay What to Whom and Why?

Your state's marital laws also determine child support. In most states, the income and ability of a parent to pay determines the amount of support.

Again, your attorney will guide you. Financial analysts like me typically get involved in the negotiation by preparing projected budgets to determine income available for support and childcare costs. The couple and their attorneys evaluate payments under various scenarios depending on who pays and how much.

Child support does not typically include private school,

extracurricular activities, or the child's first car. These costs can be negotiated and specifically included in the settlement agreement. The support a father might pay is only the support needed during his ex-wife's time with the children. In this case, the father is still responsible for child expenses when he is with the children. If he feels like he's paying support and still covering an unfair share of the children's expenses, he may be able to go back to court to claim that his support payments were diverted.

All states have specific child support guidelines, but judges have the authority to deviate from those guidelines when the situation warrants more flexibility. Parents may not be able to opt out or agree to waive child support for less than the guidelines require. Even if parents agree to joint physical custody, the wealthier or higher earning parent will probably pay child support.

Child support guidelines are based on the number of children and a corresponding percentage of the paying spouse's anticipated income from all sources. Voluntary unemployment or underemployment during divorce won't sit well with the judge. In that case, previous income may be considered. Last, the child's needs or childcare costs can impact guideline amounts.

Depending on state law, child support can be extended to age 23 if the child remains in school, or indefinitely if the child is disabled.

Let's consider Texas again. Texas uses a set of specific guidelines and formulas. Child support is typically a flat percentage of the noncustodial parent's income after allowable deductions like taxes. Child support is enforced by the attorney general, and the consequences for failure to pay include wage garnishment and possible jail time.

California, in contrast, uses *income shares tables* based on estimates of child costs. The table assumes that the child's costs reflect spending necessary to maintain or restore the child's lifestyle. An amount of each parent's income is proportionally divided.

While other, more creative terms can be negotiated in mediation or in a collaborative divorce process, these are the rules and minimum requirements a judge will look at when considering support. Attorneys can fight to get the best possible outcome by claiming special circumstances. But fighting over the cost of children is time consuming and costly. The process can eat away family financial resources. After all that fighting, there will be less money to actually provide support for the children.

One last, but important point: Spouses might try to use child or spousal support as a bargaining chip in exchange for a nonfinancial agreement. Here's an example: Bill will not give Jane additional support unless she agrees that Bill's girlfriend may "sleep over" when the children stay with him on the weekends. In my opinion, this is blackmail, especially when the recipient spouse really needs the additional financial support. While financial issues always have an emotional component, using money (especially money used to support children) to gain nonfinancial agreement on adult issues is just not cool. Try to negotiate other solutions first. Maybe Jane's boyfriend can "sleep over." Unfortunately, I can't promise you that this won't happen. You may have to give up something nonfinancial to get the money you need to get to a workable agreement.

Child and Alimony Support Payments: Taxes

Child support payments you receive are not taxable, but alimony payments could be. The spouse paying support pays child support with after-tax dollars but, for agreements struck before December 31, 2018, gets a deduction for alimony payments if structured correctly according to IRS rules. Simple, right? Wrong. The IRS doesn't hand out deductions without strict limits to avoid abuse. As always, the devil is in the details!

Because of their special tax status, alimony payments awarded before December 31, 2018 can be structured to conserve family income by reducing combined taxes. This works well in situations when the paying spouse is in a much higher tax bracket postdivorce. However, under the new tax laws, called the Tax Cuts and Jobs Act of 2017, alimony will not be deductible after December 31, 2018. The following story illustrates the impact of alimony tax deductions allowed in agreements before 2019.

Harold and Maude

Harold and Maude divorced. Harold was a highly paid corporate executive while Maude stayed home to raise their children. Maude believed that her child support payments wouldn't be enough for her to maintain anywhere close to her previous *lifestyle. She wanted $8,000 a month in alimony in addition to child support. Harold thought that was a little too much. Harold's financial analyst showed Harold that he would actually pay Maude only $6,000. Here's how it worked. Harold paid Maude $10,000 a month in tax-deductible alimony. Because Harold was in the highest tax bracket (almost 40 percent), the real after-tax expense was only $6,000. Maude, who was in the 20 percent tax bracket, received $8,000 a month after taxes.*

Too bad for the IRS. In this scenario, the IRS lost $2,000 a month since otherwise Harold would have paid $4,000 in taxes on the same $10,000. Does anyone feel sorry for the IRS?

Alimony is not child support, so keep the two separate in negotiations. For divorce agreements made before midnight December 31, 2018, the IRS could change the tax status of the payment if alimony stops on any date related to the child, like graduation from high school. There are also IRS recapture rules for alimony when alimony increases or decreases significantly in the first three years. This is a complicated rule and many attorneys are not aware of it, so have a CPA or CDFA® review planned alimony before you sign your divorce decree.

Last, the term and amount of support payments can impact the ability to refinance an existing mortgage or get a new mortgage once the divorce is final. These rules change periodically, but support payments may be considered income to qualify for a mortgage. If a mortgage or refinancing will be required post-divorce, be prepared before you sign your decree. Find a divorce

mortgage professional in your area at www.divorcelendingasso-
ciation.com.

Final Thoughts

Child support and alimony are legal concepts. The application of
these concepts requires an attorney, a CPA, and a financial analyst with experience in divorce. While family and friends might
offer good counsel, they also may have their own agendas and
could do harm. Experts can provide valuable assistance, including an assessment of the income used to determine payments or
the cost of your standard of living.

Knowledgeable financial professionals will help make the
case for support. However, it's your attorney, a mediator, or a
judge who will help you negotiate or decide who will pay what
to whom.

Action Items

❏ The right to support depends on state law. Find out more at
   www.divorcesource.com.

❏ Consult a CPA or CDFA® before finalizing any settlement
   that includes deductible alimony payments. Find one near
   you at www.institutedfa.com.

❑   Consult a mortgage broker before you divorce, especially if
    you plan to receive alimony, and apply for a mortgage after
    your divorce is final. Find a mortgage broker near you at
    www.divorcelendingassociation.com.

Taxes and Hidden Assets

IGNORING YOUR SPOUSE IS NOT A good idea. Ignoring your taxes—even worse! Failure to keep your head during divorce could lead to thousands of dollars in unexpected tax liabilities payable to Uncle Sam. Taxes impact the value of houses, investments, and retirement plans, so they may impact the relative "fairness" of your settlement.

This chapter prepares you to ask important questions about the income and wealth you will divide in divorce. It's divided into two sections. In the first, you'll learn how to find undisclosed (aka hidden) wealth by reading a tax return. In the second, you'll learn basic tax calculations used to find the after-tax value of each of your accounts and properties. Future chapters provide even more information on how taxes affect the value of particular assets, such as houses and retirement plans.

I like this stuff. But for most people, this chapter is about as fun as wet socks on a long walk. It's required reading, nonetheless.

Part I: Reading the Tax Return

If a spouse is not honest or forthcoming about money, proper analysis of a tax return can identify some (but not all) undisclosed accounts or assets.

Lynn and Mike

Lynn suspected her husband Mike was not disclosing all his income sources during their divorce. She knew that she and her husband received some sort of income from a trust, but she didn't know how much or the size of the trust. It wasn't until her financial analyst looked at their joint tax return that she saw the actual income from a trust.

There are many different types of trusts, and each is unique in some way—with different rules regarding distributions and sale, and how income is taxed. Even if a trust is inherited and therefore separate property, the income from it might matter. Depending on state law, the income benefit from the trust may be a marital asset or a factor in determining support.

Bruce and Shana

Bruce believed that his wife, Shana, had no retirement plan through her job as a floral assistant at a local flower shop. He assumed this fact because the shop was small. However, her W-2 statement, an annual statement her company provided to her to prepare income taxes, showed that she did contribute to a plan.

The moral of both stories: Tax documents provide a significant amount of information. But as riveting as they may be, you must look beyond the tax return. Only income-producing employment, accounts, and property appear on the tax return. Other sources of money may be found in noninterest bearing checking accounts, older retirement plans, certain *capital gain* investments like land, some corporate benefits, etc. You'll need a credit report, a financial analyst, and an attorney in addition to your own intuition to find these hidden gems.

Note: Tax returns are prepared to minimize income so that the payer can pay as little as possible to the IRS. You'll need a CPA or financial analyst to reverse deductions and exemptions in order to get to actual income earned, which is then used to calculate support.

THE ABCs OF TAXES AND HIDDEN ASSETS

For most taxpayers, the tax year is the same as the calendar year. Taxpayers file by April 15, 2019, for the 2018 tax year. Taxes must be paid by then, although the filing deadline can be extended to October. Trusts and businesses have different filing deadlines.

Tax returns are filed on behalf of individuals, married couples (who can file jointly or separately), and head of household (for single filers that support dependents like children or even other adults). Each has its own tax rate and rules regarding exemptions and deductions.

In order to file taxes as a married couple for a given year, you must be married by midnight on December 31 of that year. If you divorce before year's end, you will file as a single person or a head of household if your children (or others) are with you and supported by you more than half the year. In the year of and in the years after divorce, you may want to keep a calendar of when the children are with you in order to qualify for head-of-household status, which offers a larger standard deduction from income and better marginal tax rates. A CPA or CDFA® can help you evaluate your options. In the year of divorce, the total tax expense may be greater than or less than filing as a married couple. Sometimes the difference is significant enough to change the anticipated date of divorce from December to January. A CPA or tax accountant can estimate the difference.

Taxpayers, other than trusts and some businesses, file their taxes on a form called the 1040 or 1040A. The forms discussed below provide information to prepare the 1040 and 1040A tax return.

The W-2

For salaried employees, annual earnings and federal tax withholding appear in a tax statement called the W-2. The W-2 also shows contributions to company retirement plans, income from stock options, etc. Each item reported has its own code, and codes can be found on the IRS website or at www.w-2 instructions.com/.

The withholding rate varies for each employee, and the employee can determine the rate. Withholding too much will result in a tax refund or in money held *on deposit* at the IRS for future taxes. In the year of divorce, a spouse could purposely withhold too much in order to "hide" money from a spouse. A CDFA® or CPA can easily find this overpayment by reviewing the tax return. Spouses may agree to divide tax refunds in the year of divorce, but when you need access to cash immediately, you may need to pursue other options, like direct compensation for overpayment at settlement.

The 1099 Statement

The 1099 is similar to a W-2. There are several forms, but each shows income from a specific source of income, like earnings from work as an independent contractor, income and taxable gains from an investment account, or distributions from government payments.

The K-1

The K-1 shows income from partnerships and certain types of investments that operate as a limited partnership. Like the W-2 and 1099, you include the data on the K-1 on your personal taxes. A K-1 indicates the existence of another taxable entity. You may need to look at even more forms.

WHAT DO THE 1040 AND 1040A TAX FORMS TELL YOU?

These forms can explain a lot about your family's financial resources and help identify hidden or previously undisclosed accounts. They include the following sections and supporting schedules.

In the Rearview Mirror:
Wages and Other Income Appear Smaller Than Actual Size

The first part of the return includes income from wages, investments, and businesses. These are then reduced by amounts that are never taxed. Income that is not taxed includes income used to make retirement account contributions, student loan interest, qualified moving or education expenses, and paid alimony. These and certain other reductions are subtracted from total income to arrive at an *adjusted gross income*. Some of these deductions are no longer allowable after 2017 under new tax laws called the Tax Cuts and Jobs Act of 2017.

Investment Losses May Be Marital Assets

Capital gains and losses are reported as other taxable income. Capital losses are limited to $3,000 per year, although, like other tax rules, that limit could change. A $3,000 capital loss may indicate that there is a large capital loss *carryforward*. For example, in 2008 the market fell and many investors sold (*liquidated*) the stocks and bonds in their investment portfolios. These sales created capital losses. A $100,000 loss, for example, has to be matched to capital gains in the same year. If there were no capital gains, only $3,000 of the capital loss can be used to offset other income that year. The remaining $97,000 can be used to offset capital gains in the future. Since a loss carryforward can be valuable to offset future capital gains, it is typically divisible in divorce. The total amount of the capital loss carryforward can be found on Schedule D, described below.

Exemptions and Deductions Have Stories to Tell, Too

This part of the tax return includes all personal exemptions and deductions. Each family member gets one personal exemption ($4,050 in 2017). However, the personal exemption is suspended for tax returns starting December 31, 2017, and until December 31, 2025, under new tax laws called The Tax Cut and Jobs Act of 2017. In divorce, up until the new tax laws take effect in 2018, the exemptions for children could be traded between the parties or awarded to the custodial parent. Exemptions reduce the adjusted gross income and so reduce taxes. Adjusted gross income is further reduced by deductions. Certain deductions may be itemized on Schedule A. If total itemized deductions (medical expenses, property taxes, mortgage interest, and charitable giving) are not large enough, a *standard deduction* may be elected instead. In 2018, the standard deduction is greatly increased while itemized deductions have been eliminated or are more limited than before. The amount of the standard deduction for single filers for 2018 is $12,000, up from $6,350 in 2017. For married couples, the standard deduction is $24,000 up from $12,700. For someone with high income, exemptions and deductions are valuable.

This section can reveal wasted or hidden cash that can be

divided in divorce. Higher-than-average (or lower-than-average) deductions of any kind in the year leading up to divorce are red flags that require investigation. For example, a much lower mortgage interest deduction could indicate that the mortgage has been *paid down*. A soon-to-be ex might use joint savings to pay off the mortgage debt and leave an unsuspecting spouse with much less cash, forcing that spouse to sell the house that he or she loves but can no longer afford.

Hiding in Plain Sight:
Taxes Previously Withheld and Tax Credits

There are many ways your spouse can hide money that only a private investigator may find. If you're married to someone who stashes money above the ceiling tiles in your bathroom or under floorboards or behind a heat vent, you'll need more help than a financial analyst. A financial analyst *can* find hidden money on the tax return. One way your spouse could hide assets is by leaving money deposited at the IRS.

If you see a positive number in the *refund* section of your most recent tax return, *pay attention*. Taxpayers can apply a refund (meaning an overpayment) to future years. Any overpayment belongs on your list of assets. An IRS overpayment may be a marital asset divisible in divorce.

Credits for education, dependent care, energy, and foreign taxes, if allowed, follow exemptions and deductions on the return. While exemptions reduce income, credits directly reduce your tax expense. In divorce, some of these credits must be allocated to the parent with custodial responsibilities. Consult your CPA or tax preparer to determine if you can take these valuable credits.

Where to Look: Tax Schedules

Schedules attached to the tax return reveal more details. The most common schedules are as follows (although the presentation of these on the tax form can change):

Schedule A lists itemized deductions mentioned under Exemptions and Deductions above.

Schedule B reports taxable interest or ordinary dividends. This schedule lists accounts that generate either interest or dividends. Income from an unfamiliar account or investment may appear here. Ask your attorney to put down his latté and look into this.

Schedule C reports income or loss from a business you operated. An activity qualifies as a business if your primary purpose for engaging in the activity is for income or profit and you are involved in the activity with "continuity and regularity." For example, if your spouse is a massage therapist and she works under her own name, she might report her business's income and expenses on this schedule. A business owner might delay sales contracts, inflate expenses, or prepay expenses if he or she sees divorce on the horizon in order to appear as if his or her income declined.

Schedule D reports the sale or exchange of capital assets, gains from involuntary conversions of capital assets, capital gain distributions, and nonbusiness bad debts. Like Schedule B, this may reveal previously unreported assets or accounts. In addition, Schedule D may indicate that there are valuable accumulated investment losses (capital losses) to divide in a divorce and use to offset investment gains (capital gains) in future years for one or both spouses.

Schedule E reports income or loss from rental real estate, royalties, partnerships, S corporations, estates, trusts, and so on. Much of the information needed for schedule E comes from other tax returns. Consider hiring a CPA or financial analyst to review this section and the records used to prepare it.

Tax returns from closely held businesses reveal important information. Look into income shown on tax forms 1099 or K-1. Like individual returns, business tax returns should be analyzed over several years. A large increase in cash, inventory, or even accounts receivable on the balance sheet of a business could indicate hidden cash in the business, or it might just mean that the business is changing. Look for sudden changes like these, and point them out to your attorney, CPA, and financial analyst.

Part II: Basic Tax Concepts

As you know by now, divorce may not be "fair," but we can try to get to a workable solution. When dividing assets, the negotiation will be based not only on economic factors but also on emotion and emotion's cousin, convenience. This section addresses the economics, but other considerations can be just as important for getting to a workable solution.

To divide money from income, investments, and property fairly from an economic standpoint, you need to know their true after-tax values. The following tax concepts will help you understand how to assess the value of your settlement.

TAX BASIS

Before you agree to any division of property, determine the tax basis (or cost basis) of all of the family's investments and property. Tax basis is the original purchase price of the investment and is sometimes adjusted under IRS rules. The tax basis is subtracted from the sales price in order to establish taxable capital gains or losses on investments. The tax basis determines the tax expense of selling an investment or property and impacts the choices you have when dividing them in divorce.

Retirement accounts and the family home are a family's two largest assets. Retirement accounts have no basis—all withdrawals in retirement are taxed—because taxpayers get a tax deduction from income each time they contribute to their retirement account (with the exception of Roth IRAs).

Homes typically have a tax basis, but the tax expense is complicated by IRS rules. For example, a home purchased twenty years ago for $100,000 is now worth $750,000. So the gain must be $650,000, right? Not necessarily. The tax basis might be $150,000—$50,000 more than the purchase price. Why? Because the couple made $50,000 of improvements to the property over the years. The IRS allows the homeowner to add improvements (but not repairs) to the basis.

The calculation of taxable gain on the home is further complicated because the IRS exempts a big part of the gain from taxes if the home is the couple's primary residence—$500,000 for couples and $250,000 for individuals. To qualify, homeowners must have owned the home for two years and lived in the home for two of the last five years.

So taxes on the sale of the home could be significantly higher (and proceeds significantly less) depending on who "owns" the home, according to the IRS rules. In the example above, the taxable gain is the $750,000 sales price less the $500,000 exemption (assuming the couple is married) less the $150,000 cost basis, for a total capital gain of $100,000. Tax is paid on the gain. If the tax rate is 15 percent, the tax expense is $15,000. By comparison, the capital gain for a single filer is the $750,000 sales price less the $250,000 exemption less the $150,000 cost basis, for a total capital gain of $350,000. If the tax rate is 15 percent, the tax expense is $52,500. The tax expense of selling in the example is $37, 500 more if you are a single filer.

If you believe that the taxable gain on the marital home exceeds $250,000, financial analysis is critical because the homeowner spouse could be subject to significantly greater taxes when she ultimately sells the home, which reduces proceeds she expects from the sale and could result in an unintentional (or intentional) settlement imbalance.

Jason and Emma

Jason and Emma were divorcing. For simplicity, each wanted to take one of the following: a $100,000 investment in land or $100,000 in cash. Emma planned to sell the land. "How much did the land cost?" I asked. It turned out that the cost basis was $10,000. If sold, Emma would face a $90,000 taxable gain on the land. The result: Emma was awarded not only the land but also cash sufficient to "equalize the estate" and compensate her for the taxes she'll need to pay when she sells it.

Other factors might be at play here. Proper financial research and analysis of capital gains will help you make more informed choices.

INCOME TAX RATES

The tax rate you'll pay impacts the value of each source of income, investment, or property. Because of different tax consequences, $100,000 of a traditional IRA account may not have the same after-tax value as a $100,000 Roth IRA account or a $100,000 investment in land or a taxable joint account.

Retirement accounts like IRAs (but not Roth IRAs) are taxed at *ordinary tax rates* upon withdrawal. Ordinary rates are also known as *marginal tax rates* of income because the higher the income, the higher the rate. Ordinary rates currently range from 0 percent to 37 percent. Joint nonretirement investment accounts and land are taxed at capital gain rates, and only the gain (sales price less purchase price) is taxed at that rate. Withdrawals from a Roth IRA are not taxed, although there are exceptions. Withdrawals from retirement accounts like IRAs before age 59 ½ incur an additional 10 percent penalty, although (again) there are exceptions and these rules are subject to change.

Marginal rates are paid on income, such as your salary, interest earned, or withdrawals from most retirement accounts. The marginal rate is *progressive*. For example, someone who is single and in the "22 percent marginal tax bracket" and has taxable income of $24,525 per year may pay a 12 percent tax on the first $9,525, and 22 percent on the remaining $15,000. Thus, anyone whose income is in the 22 percent marginal tax bracket pays a lower overall tax rate (called the *effective rate* or weighted average tax). In this case, the effective tax rate is 18.1 percent. Taxpayers also pay payroll taxes on salary income, which pays toward Social Security and Medicare benefits and is shown on your W-2. If a CPA or tax advisor prepares your taxes, the effective rate is calculated for you as part of the return. If not, simply divide taxes by your taxable income on the tax return.

Why is this important? In divorce, the highest marginal rate and/or the effective rate are assumed in many calculations to validate (or manipulate) the value of accounts. This is called *tax affecting* the value of investments. More on that later.

CAPITAL GAINS TAX RATES

The capital gains tax is only applied to the *gain* or the difference between the sale price and purchase price, which is also known as the tax basis or cost basis on the investment. Short-term capital gain rates are the same as the marginal or ordinary rates described above. Long-term capital gains rates, 15 percent (or 20 percent for high-income taxpayers), are generally assessed on gains on investments held for more than a year.

For example, if an investor buys one hundred shares of General Electric stock for $2,000 (one hundred shares of stock at $20 per share), holds it for more than a year, and then sells it for $2,500 (one hundred shares of stock for $25 per share), she is taxed on the difference between what she paid for the stock and the stock's sales price ($500, the stock's capital gain). She is taxed at long-term rates of 15 percent (or 20 percent if she has high total income). Thus, her tax is $500 × 15 percent: $75. If she held the stock for less than a year, she'd be taxed on the capital gain at ordinary rates, the same rate she pays on the rest of her taxable income.

TAX *AFFECTING* ASSETS TO BE DIVIDED IN DIVORCE

Tax affecting reduces the value of investments, retirement accounts and property during divorce negotiations by the amount the asset is taxed upon withdrawal or sale, so assuming the correct tax rate is important. The spouse receiving tax-affected assets will end up with more of other assets, so attorneys use this tool to negotiate the best outcome for their clients.

For example, an attorney might tax affect money in a retirement plan because withdrawals will ultimately be taxed. Left unchecked, the spouse receiving more of the tax-affected retirement accounts may benefit (possibly unfairly) in negotiations from the practice. Here's why: The tax rate ultimately paid on retirement accounts depends on when and how much the owner plans (or needs) to withdraw from the account and the tax rate for that spouse at the time of withdrawal. For a forty-five-year-old, the withdrawal is likely several years away. Depending on the circumstances and assumptions, today's value of the tax consequence may be very small, but an attorney might tax affect the account at his or her client's highest marginal tax rate to manipulate the outcome of the division.

An experienced financial analyst or CDFA® can help explain to your spouse, attorney, mediator, or judge why an account should be (or shouldn't be) tax affected or whether it's meaningful enough to divide assets differently.

Final Thoughts

Tax rules are complicated, ever changing, boring, and tedious. Professional analysis may reveal hidden income, investments, and property, and change your perception of the value of the wealth divided in divorce.

If you find tax rules to be as interesting as I do, you can find much more information on the Internet at www.irs.gov or www.bankrate.com.

Action Items

❏ Gather tax returns for at least the last two years. If you don't know where they are, or your soon-to-be ex won't share them, you may be able to get the information you need from the IRS. Go to www.irs.gov/uac/ How-to-Get-Your-Prior-Year-Tax-Information-from-the-IRS.

❏ You can find details about income, retirement contributions, and much more about the W-2 payroll statement at www.w-2instructions.com.

❏ Since not all accounts and property are included on the tax return, you'll want to look at a credit report, too. Go to www.annualcreditreport.com.

❏ Analyze how each asset will be taxed and the impact taxes will have on your property, investments, and retirement accounts upon sale. It may impact how you want assets divided in divorce.

❏ Beware of how tax basis, tax rates, and tax affecting impact your divorce negotiations. Rules change often, so advice is often worth the cost.

❏ Alert your attorney and financial analyst to potential hidden accounts or other assets.

8

The Family Home

THE FAMILY HOME—STUFFED TO THE RAFTERS with memories both good and bad—is likely the biggest piece of financial and emotional baggage couples carry. Keeping or selling it has consequences that reach beyond money, taxes, and budget concerns. Close relationships with families that live down the street, ties to neighborhood schools, and proximity to work are just some of the factors that complicate the decision to keep or sell.

It's not enough to keep the home because your children took their first steps there. Ignoring the economics of keeping the home may lead to the very instability you're trying to avoid. Spouses facing divorce must calculate the cost of living under two separate roofs and remain flexible as they consider the emotional and financial consequences of selling or keeping the home. You could end up house rich and cash poor.

You have a choice on how to spend your money. You could spend it on property taxes, furniture and repairs, or on bonding experiences with your children and enlightening activities for them, and you. Which of these do you think most often leads to happiness and stability?

"Perfect" Is the Enemy of "Good"

Divorcing couples should engage a real estate or leasing agent to shop for affordable housing. Most times, other houses and apartments are available in the same school district, if that's a major consideration, and it often is. But first you must determine what you both can afford.

In a perfect world (though, if it were perfect, you might not be reading this), housing expenses would be less than 25 to 30 percent of each spouse's expected postdivorce income. Housing expenses include mortgage payments, insurance, property taxes, homeowners' association fees, and maintenance. Without enough money, in as little as one year, both parties could end up regretting a decision to keep the family home or purchase a second one. And don't count on easily selling the home if things don't work out. In a difficult market environment, it may take a long time to sell at the price you want. Have at least eighteen months of housing expenses saved, because it could take that long to sell.

If you decide to keep the home, you need to decide (1) who will live in the home and for how long, and (2) whether the home will be transferred to that spouse. Whoever keeps the home will need the financial resources to pay housing expenses in addition to other living expenses, like replacing furniture and other items awarded to the other spouse.

Last, I recommend that divorcing couples hire a home inspector well before trying to negotiate a divorce settlement, to evaluate potentially costly repairs that can impact the value of the home or the cost of keeping it.

The Value of the Family Home and Other Fairy Tales

The value of your home has nothing to do with how much you love the way the oak tree in back shades the little sandbox Junior played in years ago. Junior will remember the joys of that sandbox throughout his life. Try to cast aside guilt and move on.

In divorce, the *equity* in the home gets divided, not the offer to buy or *market value*. The equity in the home is the appraised or market value of the home, less any debt (mortgages, home equity loans, or liens on the home from failure to pay contractors). The appraised value is an estimate of the sales price. It fluctuates with market conditions. An appraiser will look at recent sales in your area and add or subtract value based on your home's features. Appraisals are opinions and may differ between appraisers, sometimes significantly. Debt is subtracted from the appraised value to determine equity. Your attorney or financial analyst can (and should) request a full title search, which will show all debt secured by the home.

Irene and Steve

In her divorce, Irene got the Victorian three-story surrounded by lilacs. She had no idea that her ex-husband, Steven, opened a home equity line of credit (HELOC) on the home two years before. Irene decided to sell the home one year after the divorce. The settlement agreement never addressed the HELOC because it had a zero balance. The title search showed that her husband borrowed $50,000 under the line. She had to sue her ex-husband in court to try to recover money. At least she had the lilacs. They came in handy as aromatherapy in court.

The example above demonstrates that you need to find all debt secured by the home (using a title search) and ideally close joint lines of credit. If that's not possible, your agreement must address how and when such lines will be used, monitored, and eventually closed after divorce in your agreement.

Mortgage and credit lines are typically joint debt, so the lender may look to you when your spouse fails to pay. If you're the spouse that's moving out, ask if your agreement can require that you receive copies of all statements so if your ex misses a payment, you'll know (and have the opportunity to fix it) before the lender does. More on this later.

What Should Be an Asset Could Be an Albatross

Nearly 70 percent of families own a home, but the amount of equity in American homes is declining due to low-cost mortgages and other debt options. Imagine finding out that the debt secured by your home is as much as (or even greater than) the value of the home itself!

Dianne and Warren

Dianne never kept track of her financial situation while married to Warren, a laid-off attorney who assured Dianne they could continue to live as they had. Every request she made drew the same response. Sure, Dianne could buy the red convertible. Sure, Dianne and her mother could take a trip to Greece together. And Warren was equally generous with himself: Sure, he could have an affair with the tattooed barista at Dianne's favorite coffee shop. When they divorced, she learned that their home had been refinanced to pay for their lavish lifestyle and the barista's tattoos.

With no home equity or savings to divide, Diane left the marriage with almost nothing. Diane struggled, while Warren's career recovered and the tattooed barista . . . well, she's irrelevant, isn't she?

Dianne found out that her home was worthless in spite of her lavish lifestyle. But imagine finding out that you still owe money on the house you "lost" in your divorce—well after the divorce! In divorce, a debt secured by the home most often becomes the responsibility of the person using the home, but only in the eyes of your settlement agreement, and not in the eyes of your lender.

Jill and Bart

When Bart and Jill divorced, Bart got the house. Two years later, he was laid off and stopped making mortgage payments. Jill was surprised when their mortgage lender, Chase Bank, called to demand payment in arrears. Jill told them she'd kicked Bart's "arrears" to the curb, but Chase insisted she was still responsible for mortgage payments. Jill's credit score plummeted.

Even though the settlement agreement awarded the home to Bart, Jill was still responsible for payment in the eyes of the lender. It didn't have to end that way. (The marriage did, but the settlement didn't.) The settlement agreement could have included terms to protect Jill. The settlement could have required Bart to refinance the mortgage in his own name. And if he failed to do so within a reasonable time period, the settlement agreement could have allowed Jill to sell the home to repay the mortgage in order to relieve her of responsibility for the debt.

While some settlement agreements include refinancing provisions like this or legal protections that can be structured by an attorney like a "deed of trust to secure assumption," often the nonowner spouse doesn't know anything until the former spouse misses several payments. So how will you know? Get transparency. If your spouse gets the house, you can and should attempt to get copies of the postdivorce payments.

Note: Because divorcées live on half of what they did before, at least for the short term, I'm a big proponent of selling the home and dividing home equity in divorce instead of the strategies above. I know that selling is not always an option in all markets, but I see mortgage debt and credit lines choking family finances postdivorce. When one ex-spouse misses a mortgage payment or fails to pay property taxes, the divorce and its costs seem to start all over again. No one wants that, except for maybe a greedy attorney or an eager homebuyer looking for a fire sale.

Is the Family Home Marital or Separate Property?

Like other assets, an attorney may look at how and when you and your soon-to-be ex purchased the home and where you got the money. This will determine whether the home, or part of the home, might be considered separate property. As has been stated over and over and 'round and 'round (but can hardly be emphasized enough), it can be expensive for attorneys and their forensic accountants to make the case for separate property under the laws of each state, especially in long marriages.

Cami and James

James made the down payment on a home from money kept in a separate account at their bank—money inherited from his uncle. Cami and James used their combined income to make mortgage payments. Five years later, the couple divorced. Is the home marital property?

Division depends on state law, court precedents, or the judge. Or on who has the better attorney. In some states, depending on when the home was purchased, James could claim that the home was his separate property because he made the down payment from inherited money. A judge might award Cami half of all her mortgage payments paid to principal (not interest) on the mortgage. Alternatively, James could receive reimbursement from the marital estate for his down payment, using marital property. Whatever remains of the home equity is all that's left to divide after James is reimbursed. Or, again depending on the state you live in, a judge may decide that the home is marital property. How? An attorney might argue that the down payment was a marital gift to Cami and ask the court to equally divide all equity in the home. Or it can come down to comingling—when James deposited the down payment in a joint account before making the down payment. Each state treats these arguments differently. Your attorney is there to argue for you, but he may not convince a judge that his interpretation of the law is valid. In cases like this, you and your spouse have a clear choice. You can decide together how to divide the home or you can spend oodles of time and money sorting it out in the legal system.

The comingling of separate and marital property most often involves the marital home. If each spouse owns a home or has an investment account before marriage, buying a home together with these proceeds may cause separate property to become marital in some states, even if the contributions are unequal. And if this is you, you are not alone. The concept of marital property is a moving target and subject to interpretation. Even a small misstep may have tripped the wire from separate to marital. *This is the primary reason for a formal marital agreement, even if it's only an agreement about your investment in the home.*

Bob and Sherrie

Bob and Sherrie married. Sherrie moved out of her apartment into Bob's home, which he purchased two years earlier. Bob and Sherrie earned about the same amount at their jobs as registered nurses. Sherrie agreed to pay the $2,000 mortgage each month for ten months, so her payments would equal Bob's $20,000 down payment. At that point, they would divide the mortgage obligation. Six years later, they divorced. The home's value had doubled over the years because an old building nearby was demolished to make room for a beautiful park. However, Bob was awarded the home because he proved it was his separate property. Sherrie was awarded half of the principal payments on the mortgage. Because the largest percentage of mortgage payments in the first years of loan amortization (loan reduction) is interest and not principal, Sherri left the marriage with much, much less than she expected.

The intentions behind such informal financial agreements are good, but intentions may not be enough. Marriages can be defined by the thousands of little agreements we make with our spouses. You take out the trash, I'll do the dishes. But when it comes to agreements about the largest financial assets in our lives, and our expectation these investments will benefit us in the future, I firmly believe the agreement needs to be formal and legal. With proper planning and legal agreement, Bob and Sherrie could have agreed to co-own the home. Instead Sherrie unwittingly missed out on the home's growth in value. After significant expense, Bob "won" the legal fight in this story, but I wonder how he's sleeping at night.

The Family Home and Taxes

Under current tax law, $250,000 of the *gain* on the sale of a primary home (not a second home) is exempt from taxes for single homeowners. For married homeowners, $500,000 is exempt, as long as the home was owned for two years and occupied for two of the last five years. In addition, there may be state transfer taxes upon sale.

The gain on the home is its sale price adjusted for selling costs (such as the expense of a real estate agent) less the cost basis in the home. The cost basis is the purchase price plus the cost of improvements on the home, but not maintenance or repairs. Cost basis has nothing to do with the mortgage or how the home was financed.

The tax rules for determining gain on the sale of a home changed in 1997. Under pre-1997 rules, the IRS reduced the cost basis of a new home by the amount of gain on the sale of the old home. That had the effect of increasing the potential gain on a sale of the new home. So if the couple sold any primary residential home (not necessarily the current home) before 1997, the basis of the current home may need to be adjusted for the gain on that home. A financial analyst, CPA, or tax advisor will be able to help you sort out the implication of this rule change or any other change in tax laws for the sale of a couple's primary home.

If sale of the home would result in a capital gain in excess of $250,000, proceed with caution. Otherwise you may end up with fewer proceeds than the settlement anticipated. Consult with a tax advisor or CPA to determine the tax expense associated with the sale of the home even if the home will not be sold due to the divorce. The tax expense impacts the value of the home, and the value divided in divorce should reflect this cost.

Ellie and Herman

Ellie and Herman are divorcing. Everyone is stunned. They seem so well suited, tearing around town wearing logo-festooned bike apparel on their matching racing bikes.

At any rate, Ellie and Herman own a home with a cost basis of $100,000 that could potentially sell for $500,000 after selling costs. If they sell the home before the divorce, the $400,000 gain is exempt from taxes. But if the home is transferred to Ellie, she may have to pay taxes on the gain in excess of the $250,000 exemption for single owners when she sells it. She will be subject to taxes equaling $22,500, or 15 percent multiplied by the difference between the $400,000 gain and the $250,000 exemption. (The tax rate on capital gains is 20 percent for high-income earners.) The *transfer scenario could result in a settlement imbalance. While a settlement decree in this scenario may show the home at the net sale value of $500,000, the actual value of the asset on Ellie's side of the balance sheet should be $477,500 (less, if you include selling costs and transfer taxes).*

In this example, if Ellie takes the home and eventually sells it, she and Herman are unnecessarily wasting money on taxes. If the home is not sold before the divorce, co-ownership is an alternative option that can preserve family assets from tax. If Ellie and Herman co-owned the home, they would get the benefit of the larger tax exemption if certain conditions are met.

These are the economic variables, but emotions should be a factor in any decision to co-own the home after divorce. A settlement agreement that allows for co-ownership is often difficult in the friendliest of divorces. For example, there likely will be a requirement to "maintain" the property. Divorced spouses may argue about what maintenance is important and who should pay for it. And co-ownership of the home could take an even bigger emotional toll. What will Herman think (or do) if Ellie's new boyfriend moves in?

Sallie and Sam

Sallie and Sam purchased a home together for $125,000 just after they married. Now, fifteen years later, the mortgage is paid off, and they are getting divorced. Sallie wants to stay in the home with her teenage children. Sallie is awarded the home, *and Sam is awarded their savings account, worth an equal amount. Sam is also required to pay child support for three years. Three years later Sallie wants to sell the home, but she can't. There is no market for a sale. Sallie has little income and household bills are piling up. Banks will not lend to her because she doesn't have enough regular income. Sallie's credit card is close to maxed out, and she may be forced to sell the home well below its market value.*

With the right planning, this all could have turned out much better. In their negotiation, Sallie wanted to stay in the home with her children. Emotion and convenience won out over economics, but the economics came back to haunt her three years later. If Sallie and Sam had agreed to co-own the home, until she moved out, and divide the savings account, Sallie might have had enough savings to ride out the sale of the home. Or the couple might have agreed to sell the home three years earlier, and divide the equity and the saving account. And then budgeted for new accommodations within their means.

You Cannot Cut It into Two

Almost every prospective client tells me how they plan to divide the home. But after considering all their options, many choose a different path.

Some choose to buyout their spouse using cash from marital or separate property. When there is not enough cash to compensate the selling spouse, the buyout can also be accomplished with refinancing, an owelty lien (if eligible) or a *promissory note*. A mortgage broker with experience working with divorcing couples, a CDFA®, or an attorney should review you needs and options well before you sign a final divorce decree.

Brenda and David

Brenda and David are divorcing. They own a home worth $360,000 with a mortgage of $300,000. Brenda has significant separate property from an inheritance. Brenda agrees to stay in the home and pays David $30,000 for his share of the equity. The settlement agreement gives her six months to refinance the mortgage before David can sell the home in order to repay the mortgage. Under the settlement agreement, David transfers full title to Brenda.

This worked out for Brenda and David only because they knew Brenda was approved for the refinancing *before settlement*. This gave David confidence that the mortgage could be refinanced and he would have no responsibility for the liability postdivorce. If Brenda had not inherited the money, she could have offered David a promissory note in exchange for his share of the equity in the home. Brenda would get the house and David would get payments from Brenda on the note.

A promissory note can be drawn up by an attorney and, if possible, secured with a lien on the property. The terms are negotiated and can be specific to the needs of the couple. The note most often requires regular payment of principal and interest. Alternatively, it could require a payment in full upon a specific date or when an event such as sale of the home occurs, within a specified period. If you are considering a promissory note and lien, consult a qualified mortgage lender and CPA and know your options before you settle your divorce. In the example above, any lien on a property may, without intent, cause Brenda to be refused financing.

A promissory note has other potential drawbacks, so proceed with caution. It may be emotionally difficult to have a large financial connection to your former spouse for the period of the note. Moreover, the resident spouse may be unwilling or unable to pay the note due to disability, job loss, resentment, or simply not caring enough to bother making payments. A lawsuit may provide the only remedy, and going to court is costly, time consuming, and emotionally draining (I sound like a broken record). There are also economic drawbacks to a promissory note. In the example above, interest on the note is taxable to David, and payments may or may not be considered a source of income to David if he applies for a mortgage of his own. And if Brenda files for bankruptcy, David may not get paid, ever.

Final Thoughts

When there is a market to sell the home, I believe a sale is the best choice for everyone in divorce. If you decide to keep the home, you must be realistic about whether you will have enough cash to pay expenses—including mortgages, property taxes, insurance, and maintenance—for at least eighteen months beyond an anticipated sale. If your spouse will keep the home, you may need protection in the agreement that includes transparency about payments on liens secured on the home and the ability for you to step in and sell the home if your spouse misses payments.

Action Items

❏   Work with your CPA to determine the capital gain on the home. If there is a capital gain in excess of $250,000 (currently or anticipated), co-owning the home with restrictions may make economic sense. However, other more emotional considerations are just as important.

❏   If the settlement anticipates the sale of the home, it also must include specific timelines and a range of prices, as well as contingent plans if the home just won't sell. Contingent plans could include a redistribution of other assets between the spouses or a buyout.

❏   When there is a jointly held mortgage, the spouse leaving the home needs protection added to the settlement agreement, which may include a requirement to refinance or sell the home in order to remove liability for it.

9

Cash, Investments, Retirement Accounts, and Debt

YOU'RE MOVING ON, AND YOU PLAN to leave with your sanity and self-respect intact. You also plan to leave with the Le Corbusier lounge chair that you appreciate but she doesn't because she grew up in a La-Z-Boy family. While you're working that out, keep in mind that dividing the furniture is normally the least complicated aspect of divorce.

Today's financial instruments—investment accounts, retirement plans, mortgages, and credit cards—have their own rules regarding division, contributions, and withdrawals. Some of those rules involve penalties or fees. The sale or transfer of an investment may trigger taxes. There are also issues that must be addressed when dividing debts to protect your credit score.

We'll cover the most common issues here, with the goal of

keeping you in the game, uninjured, and ready for the next. Forget about "winning" and focus on maximizing your access to cash and minimizing taxes, fees, and penalties.

The Cash Is Always Greener on YOUR Side

Cash accounts, like bank and many savings accounts, are the simplest to divide. Dividing a cash account is costless, typically.

If you decide to divorce, you can agree to maintain the status quo and pay bills the way you have been, or you can develop a new system. If you don't think you and your spouse can manage this, a court will issue a temporary order that outlines who will pay what. As I've noted before, it is expensive to involve attorneys and the court, so try to handle this on your own. Be diligent, though. Even if your spouse sticks to the plan, you may see unexpected expenses appear on statements as the divorce progresses.

We all act differently when we're under stress. Some of us dip into Häagen-Dazs. Some of us dip into bank accounts so we can slip more often into our favorite shops. Keep track of unaccountable expenses on bank and credit card statements. You may want to prove that an unusual withdrawal only benefitted your spouse. You may be able to claim that the withdrawal "wasted" family assets and should be reimbursed to the marital estate. Keep the statement that shows the withdrawal. In fact, keep all statements going back at least two years. You may find a pattern of unusual spending.

Joan and George

During Joan's divorce, she noticed that her joint checking account included a regular withdrawal of $2,000 at the beginning of each month. Joan suspected her husband, George, was paying rent on an apartment for a girlfriend. Joan's attorney questioned George's attorney, who initially told us the cash withdrawal was for incidental expenses. But further questioning revealed that Joan's husband used the money to fund a personal savings account. His new personal savings account was added to the couple's list of marital assets.

In the example above, Joan's husband did what many people facing divorce do—hide money from spouses. The "girlfriend" was just a savings account in a boring little branch bank across town. But Joan was a "spender" and her husband was a "saver." Joan's husband thought if he "hid" some of the cash in savings, there would be less for Joan to spend.

Also, remember that bank or savings accounts are not the only source of cash. The sale of a couple's primary home becomes cash (after taxes on nonexempted gains, expenses, and needed repairs), as does the sale of jewelry or furniture. The sale of investments becomes cash after taxes on capital gains while the sale of most retirement assets becomes cash after penalties (if the seller is under age 59 1/2) and taxes.

Cash awarded in divorce helps divorcing couples start their lives over, providing money for a deposit on an apartment, down payment on a new home, or classes to jump-start a career. A cash award could also go toward an emergency fund or saving for a new home. Cash will be in the obvious places like bank accounts but also in less obvious places like investment accounts or even the sale of a home. When I review a proposed property division, I try to make sure my client will have enough cash postdivorce.

Kelly and Kevin

Kelly and Kevin divorced after twenty-two years of marriage. During the marriage, Kelly stayed home with their two boys while Kevin worked as a manager of a large corporation. The couple planned to rely on Kelly's $1.2 million separate property trust fund in retirement. Kelly never used the fund to support the family, and Kevin never saved much money. They spent every penny of Kevin's paycheck on their home and living expenses. In divorce, Kelly wanted their $400,000 home. She could afford the mortgage payments on their $325,000 mortgage balance as well as other expenses. Kevin left the marriage with $75,000 of retirement savings. It was an even split. Kelly got the value of the home equity worth $75,000, and Kevin got the retirement account worth $75,000. However, a month later Kevin got a pink slip. Kevin had to liquidate part of his retirement savings (paying taxes and significant penalties in the process) to cover expenses while searching for another job.

Divorce isn't fair, but perhaps Kelly and Kevin could have planned a different but workable solution in happier times. Like Mark and Laura in chapter two, Kelly and Kevin could have agreed years earlier to transfer some of the trust to marital property to protect Kevin. Or Kevin might have been able to negotiate in divorce (depending on the trust's terms) that Kelly use part of her separate property trust to buy him out of their home equity and divide the retirement account. With the cash, Kevin could have avoided the taxes and penalties he faced when he withdrew part of his retirement account. But Kevin just wanted it all to be over as fast as possible. His pride stopped him from broaching the subject with Kelly. He didn't even consider the consequences of losing his job, until it was too late.

Nonretirement Investment Accounts

Most nonretirement brokerage and investment accounts typically hold stocks, bonds, mutual funds, and annuities. With agreement, the divorce decree will define the percentage of the account to be divided. Most taxable (nonretirement) investments in joint or individual brokerage accounts are divided *in kind* with no tax consequence. For example, if the account holds 500 shares of IBM stock and is divided fifty-fifty, the wife gets 250 shares moved to her individual account and the husband gets 250 shares moved to his. The couple then closes the joint account.

You can't call foul, generally speaking, when dividing an account by percentages. If the investments in the account rise or fall before its division postdivorce, then both spouses win or lose money equally. This is called taking *market* risk. During the recession in 2008 and for a time thereafter, many spouses asked their attorneys to negotiate for specific dollar amounts instead of percentages in order to avoid market risk.

Some investments, like annuities, may have special provisions with respect to division due to divorce. Penalties or other fees may apply. Carefully review the terms of each investment before negotiation or the final decree, as these expenses impact account value.

Couples save thousands of dollars by undertaking proper financial analysis of investment accounts before creating a settlement proposal. If one of you will be in a much lower tax bracket after divorce, consider moving high-tax (low cost basis) investments to the spouse in the lower bracket. More money is conserved for spousal division, and the IRS gets less.

High-tax investments include investments that have *unrealized* capital gains and are taxed when sold. Unrealized capital gains are realized when the investment is sold. For example, if the account held IBM stock that originally cost $1,000 and is now worth $3,000, the capital gain of $2,000 will be taxed upon sale. Before sale, the $2,000 is an unrealized gain.

A CDFA® or financial analyst should review the division not only for tax reasons or liquidity (how quickly an investment can be converted into cash) but also to avoid confusion postdivorce.

Mike and Linda

During the last hours of mediation, Mike insisted that the decree state that he and his wife, Linda, move $60,000 of each spouse's share of their $1 million joint investment account to accounts for their children's future college education. Linda was awarded 60 percent of the joint account, but the language in the final decree left us unsure how to proceed. We had two options:

1. *We could divide the account first.*
   - *Linda would take 60 percent of the joint account or $600,000. Linda would then move $60,000 of investments to an account intended for the children, leaving her with $540,000.*
   - *Mike would get $400,000 (40 percent) of the joint account and move $60,000 to an account intended for the children, leaving him with $340,000.*

   Or

2. *Mike and Linda could take $120,000 out of the joint account and move it to the children's account first and then divide the remainder of the account.*
   - *Linda would get 60 percent of the remaining account or only $528,000 (60 percent of $880,000).*
   - *Mike would get $352,000 (40 percent of $880,000).*

The first option obviously favored Linda and the second favored Mike. Without *specific* instructions, this couple's settlement was headed back to mediation or court unless they could agree to split the difference. By now, you know what that means. Fortunately, in this particular case, we amicably resolved the matter with the couple's attorneys. But, until we did, both spouses experienced unnecessary stress.

It's also important to understand what documents and signatures you'll need to divide joint accounts or transfer accounts before signing your final agreement. Get required signatures from your soon-to-be ex-spouse before or when you both sign the final decree. Otherwise you'll be spending money and time trying to track him or her down well after the divorce. Your bank's website should have the requirements listed, but don't be surprised if these instructions are incomplete. You may have to call for specific instructions for your accounts.

Retirement Accounts

While the division of marital property is generally governed by state domestic relations law, any assignment of employee retirement interests might also require compliance with federal law: the Employee Retirement Income Security Act of 1974 (ERISA) and the Internal Revenue Code of 1986 (the Code). It is important to know your specific type of retirement plan (e.g., 401(k), 403b, IRA, Roth IRA), as each type of plan is treated differently.

Individual Retirement Accounts (traditional IRAs), Roth IRAs, and 401(k)s are all retirement acccounts. The Internal Revenue Service allows these accounts to grow without being taxed until you withdraw from them. Most retirement plans do not allow withdrawals without stiff penalties until you are 59 ½ years old.

Retirement plans exist to encourage savings. Because of the tax advantages associated with these plans, the IRS requires that certain rules be met before dividing retirement accounts in divorce. Do the wrong thing and the IRS will subject your share of the account to taxes and penalties.

Certain retirement accounts, such as employee 401(k) plans and company pension plans, are referred to as *qualified*, meaning they are entitled to favorable terms or tax treatment, provided these plans meet specific requirements set by the ERISA and the IRS. The division of a qualified plan requires a court order called a Qualified Domestic Relations Order ("QDRO," pronounced qua-dro). IRAs and Roth IRAs are nonqualified and can typically be divided with a signature from the owner spouse and a valid copy of the final decree.

Hundreds or even thousands of dollars are wasted in divorce because many attorneys don't know whether or not a QDRO was needed or how to prepare an accurate one. The plan administrator may refuse to abide by a QDRO unless it is in the correct form. So before your divorce is final, contact the plan administrator or the company that manages the account and ask: "What are the plan administrator's requirements and cost to divide the plan subject to divorce?" While these rules can change and plans are unique, you may want to consider consultation with a QDRO specialist. More on that later.

When deciding which accounts you want to keep in divorce, keep in mind that you cannot withdraw your share of most retirement plans without taxes and penalties until you are more than 59 ½ years old. Also, even if you are older than 59 ½, any amount you withdraw is immediately reduced by taxes (except Roth IRAs). By comparison, for nonretirement accounts (investment accounts), only the gains (the difference between the purchase price and sales price) on withdrawals are taxed, and withdrawals may be made at any age. Again, and it is worth repeating, these "rules" can and do change often. Consult with a financial planner or CDFA® before negotiating your divorce, and at least before dividing or moving accounts.

401(K) RETIREMENT PLANS

Many companies offer 401(k) retirement savings plans to their employees. These plans are qualified plans governed by the ERISA and must be divided by a QDRO. By contributing to a 401(k), employees get both tax-free earnings and often a bonus from the employer called a match. Employees may contribute earned income up to a limited amount ($18,500 per year in 2018 for anyone under the age of fifty, but $24,500 for people fifty years old and over) through an automatic reduction of their pretax earnings. Many companies *match* a portion of the employee's contribution. For example, if the employee contributes 6 percent of his salary into the plan, the employer might give the employee a *match*, a matching amount of money equal to 3 percent of the employee's salary. This bonus payment encourages employees to save. The match may *vest*, meaning the employee has a legal right to the match over time, or the employee match might vest immediately. This complicates 401(k) transfers in divorce.

Employees cannot withdraw from their 401(k)s without penalty until they leave the company, move (roll) the 401(k) to an IRA (discussed later in this chapter), and become 59 ½ years old.

As discussed earlier in this chapter, qualified retirement accounts, like 401(k)s, must be divided in divorce by the court through a special order called a Qualified Domestic Relations Order ("QRDO"). A QDRO gives specific instructions to a retirement plan administrator on how to divide a retirement account according to the terms of the divorce. The nonemployee spouse is referred to as an *alternate payee*, and his or her QDRO is the only means by which an alternate payee may acquire his or her portion of a qualified retirement account during divorce.

Your attorney should complete the QDRO before the decree is made final and submit the QDRO to the court along with the divorce decree. A QDRO provides the alternate payee an opportunity to withdraw money from the plan before age 59 ½ without the 10 percent penalty when the withdrawal is *incident to divorce*.

However, the 401(k) administrator will withhold 20 percent for taxes on any withdrawals, since taxes still need to be paid. Because each plan is different, contact the administrator of the plan to determine how your plan allows for cash distribution without penalty before you sign the final decree.

While your attorney can prepare the QDRO, consider using a QDRO specialist with experience dividing qualified plans. A QDRO specialist is typically an experienced attorney who, along with the help of a financial planner or Certified Divorce Financial Analyst, can sort through the best options to divide and value the plan based on the plan's unique terms and your needs.

It makes sense to use a specialist because qualified plans like 401(k) or pension plans are often managed by third-party administrators (or administrators hired from outside the company offering the plan). These third-party folks provide family law attorneys with standardized QDROs based on the plan, and standardized QDROs may not include all options. You want to know *all* the options available to you—not just some. Without a specialist, you stand to lose thousands of dollars.

Generally speaking, a 401(k) plan allows the *alternate payee* (the nonemployee spouse) to choose any investment available inside the plan. Your spouse's investment choices inside the 401(k) may fit you as poorly as that Le Corbusier (or La-Z Boy) lounge chair. Perhaps you're averse to any risk, and want different choices. Changing investments inside the plan will not trigger taxes. An alternate payee could also choose to move (*roll*) his or her share of the spouse's 401(k) to his or her own IRA without penalty or tax.

A nonemployee spouse has sixty days to move the money withdrawn from the alternate payee account inside a 401(k) plan to an IRA account at a bank or investment firm, or he or she could do a direct rollover of the 401(k) to an IRA account. If done correctly, this process is not subject to tax or penalty, and may increase the payee spouse's range of investment choices and reduce expenses. Of course, these rules can change.

What if your spouse borrowed against his 401(k)? It's not always easy to spot such a loan on a 401(k) statement. I cannot stress how important it is to look to see whether the account includes a loan.

Because of the high cost of this type of loan, a 401(k) loan is generally a bad idea—divorce or not. Any loans become due and payable if the employee quits or is laid off, and he or she loses the benefit of compounding account growth on a larger balance. If the employee cannot pay the 401(k) loan, the loan is considered a withdrawal that triggers taxes and penalties, although there are some limited exceptions (for example, a layoff over age fifty-five may avoid penalties on previous loans in the plan). Like other withdrawals before retirement, these withdrawals are taxed at the employee's ordinary tax rates and come with a *10 percent penalty. That's a pricy loan.*

Under the QDRO, a 401(k) loan can be deducted from either spouse's share or both shares of the 401(k) account, depending on how the loan is divided under the decree. But regardless of the division, the employee spouse continues to pay the loan.

Lee and Nancy

Lee and Nancy borrowed $15,000 from Lee's 401(k) account to buy a Subaru Outback for Nancy. Nancy thought the uber-cool Subaru would compensate for Lee's predictably stodgy Chrysler sedan. When they divorced, the couple wanted Nancy to keep the car and make loan payments. Because the employee spouse (Lee) would continue to pay the loan, the attorneys structured a contractual note in which Nancy "borrowed" $15,000 from Lee and was bound to pay Lee an amount equal to his 401(k) loan payments until the debt balance was zero.

Because of the circumstances, this was one of the best solutions for Lee and Nancy. However, if Lee were laid off or left the firm, the balance of the loan would be due and payable within a short period of time. If Lee did not have sufficient cash to pay the loan, the loan balance would become a withdrawal with taxes and penalties due. As there was no provision in their agreement to cover this, Lee would be responsible for all taxes and penalties.

Contractual loans in divorce are good for some but not for others. What if a spouse fails or refuses to pay? The only recourse is the court. However, in the case above, Lee felt confident that Nancy would be able and willing to pay to keep her Subaru—or even to sell it if the loan became due and payable.

INDIVIDUAL RETIREMENT PLANS

Traditional IRAs are another type of retirement account. Permitted contribution limits are lower compared to 401(k)s—$5,500 in 2018, or $6,500 if the contributor is fifty years old or older.

The value of the traditional IRA in your divorce may seem high, even though IRAs have such low contribution limits. Why? An employee can roll over his or her 401(k) retirement plan, which has much higher contribution limits, to an IRA when the employee leaves his or her employment with the employer who sponsored the plan. If done properly (within IRA rollover rules), the employee spouse has no tax consequence as a result of the change.

You cannot withdraw money held in a traditional IRA without taxes and a 10 percent penalty until age 59 ½. When money is withdrawn after age 59 ½, the full amount of the withdrawal is taxed at *ordinary* (marginal) *tax rates* based on the owner's income. If you need cash from an IRA before age 59 ½, there may be a way to withdraw without penalties due to certain exceptions. You can explore your options with your CDFA® or CPA.

Traditional IRA contributions are typically deducted from income on your tax return, which shields that income from taxes. However, since the IRS eventually wants its taxes, IRA owners must withdraw a portion of the IRA each year starting the April after the year the owner turns 70 ½ year old. This is called an IRA *required minimum distribution* (RMD). The RMD amount is based on the owner's actuarial age and increases each year as the owner ages.

An inherited IRA is a variation of a traditional IRA. An

inherited IRA belongs to the beneficiary of an IRA. Generally speaking an inherited IRA is separate property. However, a divorcing couple may try to use the account to equalize an estate in divorce. Unfortunately, an inherited IRA cannot be divided without tax consequence to the beneficiary. Consult a tax advisor, CPA or CDFA® if an inherited IRA is part of your negotiation. An inherited IRA may also have RMDs. If RMDs are withdrawn from your or your spouse's IRA before divorce, consult a CPA or CDFA® before dividing it.

Roth IRAs have the same contribution limits as traditional IRAs. However, Roth IRA contributions are made with nondeductible after-tax dollars, and contributions can only be made in full by those with modified adjusted gross incomes below $120,000 for single taxpayers and $189,000 for married taxpayers in 2018.

Roth IRAs have rules for withdrawals, but unlike IRAs, Roth IRAs do not have required minimum distributions for the owner. Roth IRA owners can withdraw contributions at any time, but earnings can only be withdrawn without taxes and penalties after the funds have been invested for at least five years and the owner meets one of the following requirements—the owner is at least 59 ½ years old, the owner becomes disabled, or the owner requires the withdrawal to purchase a first home.

You may not need a QDRO when dividing a traditional IRA (or Roth IRA). Depending on where the account is held (Chase, Fidelity, or Charles Schwab, for example), it may be divided with a letter of instruction or a signature guarantee from the owner spouse, and an original copy of the decree. Because rules can change, it's important to understand what you'll need for each account before signing your final agreement. Again, get required signatures from your soon-to-be ex-spouse upon signing the final decree. Otherwise you'll be trying to track him or her down well after the divorce. And, as the next example shows, there are even more considerations.

Marcia and Dan

Marcia and Dan divorced. Their decree stated that they equally split Dan's Individual Retirement Account (IRA) held at Chase Bank. Marcia dillydallied for two months before she asked her financial advisors to help her divide the account. By that time, two high-risk stock investments inside the IRA lost 50 percent of their value.

While both Marcia and Dan suffered equally, Marcia could have avoided the loss. If she or her financial advisor thought the stocks in the account were risky, Marcia could have asked for a dollar amount equal to half the account at the time of divorce instead of a percentage. Or Marcia, through her attorney, could have asked that Dan sell the investment during the divorce in order to preserve the value in the account. Since investments sold to create cash were inside the IRA, this change would have had no tax consequence, since there was no withdrawal.

In divorce, Spouse A transfers a percentage of his (or her) IRA account to Spouse B. This can be accomplished without taxes by transferring the amount into Spouse B's existing IRA or a new IRA. Spouse A can transfer investments *or* sell the investment into cash and then transfer the cash—with no tax consequence to Spouse A or B, as long as the transfer is a direct rollover or other requirements are met.

Complicated? Confused? Investment accounts and retirement accounts are basically booby-trapped with taxes and penalties. There are many attorneys who are knowledgeable about investments, but it's not possible for the majority of attorneys to keep up with the ever-evolving investment universe. Don't pay for their learning curve. Adding a qualified financial analyst like a CDFA® or CPA and planning ahead will save you thousands of dollars in the long run.

Till Debt Do Us Part

Any property distribution should also take into account how you'll handle marital debts. A simple assignment of the debts to one spouse or the other in the divorce decree may work, but it may not, depending on the nature of the debts. You may have to renegotiate with a lender or other creditor to remove a spouse's name from a debt assigned to the other. Otherwise the lender may look to both spouses for payment, regardless of what the decree says.

AUTO LOANS

Auto loans are usually allocated in divorce to the spouse who plans to keep the car. The name on the auto loan matters more than your agreement because auto lenders don't care what your decree says. If your spouse's car loan is in your name, you may be able to negotiate to have your spouse refinance the loan within a reasonable period of time. At the very least, have access to statements that evidence your ex's payments. While this is not the ideal solution, you'll have the chance to make the payment yourself in order to protect your own credit.

CREDIT CARDS

There are three ways to own a credit card:

1. Owner-held card. Only the owner of the card can use the card. This person is responsible to the issuer (for example, Chase Visa or Citibank MasterCard) for payment. He or she builds (or ruins) his or her credit history if payments are made (or not made) on time.

2. Owner-held card with authorized signatory. Both the owner and authorized signatory can use the card. In the issuer's eyes, only the owner is responsible for payment. Only the owner builds (or ruins) his or her own credit history if payments are made (or not made) on time.

3. Jointly held cards. Both owners use the card and are responsible to the issuer for payment. Both build (and ruin) their credit histories if payments are made (or not made) on time.

The first thing many attorneys do is tell the working spouse to "cut" the nonworking spouse off the credit cards. If you read the first part of this book, you'll already know the benefit of having a card in your own name before divorce is even a possibility. Apply for a credit card *before* you file for divorce (ideally). Use it sparingly and pay on time.

In divorce, if you are the authorized user, it's still best practice to pay for what you charge. (You wanted the expensive, original Le Corbusier—you pay for it.) However, the issuer will only go after the owner of the card for repayment. In a community property state such as Texas, all debt in divorce is joint debt. If you are the authorized user, the divorce court will hold you responsible for the debt, but the card issuer will still look to the account owner for payment.

Should you close joint accounts? Yes. Pay off the balance with available cash by the time you sign a final agreement and close the account. If you can't pay off the card using marital funds, transfer the balance each of you is responsible for in the settlement to cards in your own names and close the joint card. Why? Because the issuer doesn't care what your divorce decree says. To the issuer, your debt is still a joint responsibility.

But be aware that there are consequences to closing a joint account. Closing a joint account reduces access to credit, which, in turn, increases your *utilization rate*. Here's how it works. Say total available credit from two cards is $40,000 ($20,000 per card) and you have $10,000 outstanding (borrowed) on one card. That's a 25 percent utilization rate. If you close the other card, your utilization rate is 50 percent. A higher utilization rate means a lower credit score.

Account owners should remove authorized users from the card after the divorce. Many divorcing card owners remove a spouse well before divorce, leaving their spouses with no access to credit, so if you are the authorized user, be sure you have your own card before this happens. The authorized user can also request to be taken off the account.

We ask our postdivorce clients to call all credit card companies and make sure they are the only ones listed on their accounts. One year after divorce, your credit report will show your remaining accounts. You can access your report at www.annualcreditreport.com.

MORTGAGES

Like credit card companies and other lenders, mortgage lenders don't know or care what your divorce decree says. Typically, both spouses are responsible until the mortgage is refinanced by one spouse or the other or the home is sold and the mortgage is paid off.

The spouse who continues to live in the family home after divorce may be required to refinance the mortgage within a certain period of time. But he or she can refinance only if he or she can qualify for a mortgage. While court-ordered alimony or child support may count toward the income requirement for mortgages, the lender will consider not only the amount but also the tenure. Liens against the home, such as a spouse's claim to the property upon sale, will also impact the ability to get refinanced. If you plan ahead, consider refinancing under only one name prior to divorce, which may be easier than refinancing after the divorce. Before taking any step, talk to a qualified lender, such as a Certified Divorce Lending Professional (www.divorcelendingassociation.com), to make sure you can refinance *before* you sign the final decree.

As discussed in chapter eight, if refinancing (or selling) the home is not possible or practical, an attorney may structure a solution in the final decree that can protect your interests.

Bess and Ron

Bess was awarded the couple's downtown condo in her divorce. The couple purchased the condo a year earlier with a new mortgage secured by the couple's home in the suburbs. The court held Bess's husband Ron responsible for all mortgage payments. However, because her financial analyst knew Bess would still be responsible for the mortgage in the eyes of the lender, she made sure the decree required Ron to refinance the mortgage in his name and that Bess receive evidence of payment until he did. In addition, the decree stated that if he does not refinance and he misses a payment, Bess can sell the suburban home to repay the mortgage.

Better than Jill and Bart in chapter eight, but still not the ideal solution. The best way to get your name off the loan is to sell the home. Here's why: If Ron fails to pay, he negatively impacts Bess's credit score. But with the information from the mortgage statements, if Ron failed to make a payment, Bess could pay and then at least *attempt* to start the process of selling the home immediately to salvage some of her own credit.

Debts on Nonretirement Investment and 401(k) Accounts

Investors can take out loans called margin loans or Pledged Asset Lines (PALs). These loans may not be tracked by credit reporting companies like Equifax or TransUnion. Evidence of these loans appears on consolidated investment statements and can be difficult to find. A financial advisor or CDFA® can help you identify if these loans exist and how they may impact your list of marital assets.

401(k) loans are borrowed against an employee's 401k account. As described above, any loans become due and payable if the employee quits or is laid off. If the employee cannot pay the 401(k) loan, the loan is considered a withdrawal that triggers taxes and penalties, although there are some limited exceptions (for example, a layoff over age fifty-five may avoid penalties on previous loans in the plan). Like other withdrawals before retirement (age 59 1/2), these withdrawals are taxed at the employee's ordinary marginal tax rates and come with a *10 percent penalty.* The employee pays back this type of debt postdivorce, but the value can be a shared liability by either offsetting the liability with other property or assets or, as in the case of Lee and Nancy above, a promissory note due to the employee spouse.

Enlightenment Is Near

Congratulations! You made it through one of the most difficult chapters in the book. Pour yourself a glass of wine, a shot of bourbon, a cup of tea, or all three, and settle into that easy chair you love.

It's not exactly easy-breezy in the chapters ahead, but you might notice a bit of light at this point. Keep reading.

Final Thoughts

In divorce, cash is king and investments are complicated. Tax and retirement plan rules change, and the changes may impact your division, the value you receive, and your future financial security. A CDFA® and/or CPA can save you thousands of dollars by reviewing your assets and proposed division.

Action Items

❏ Divide assets so that each spouse has access to cash and a minimum of debt after you sign the decree.

❏ Have a CDFA® or CPA review your proposed division to be sure you have access to cash and that tax consequences are minimized.

❏ The division of money and value in a marriage is highly dependent on the values used. Properly value all property, accounts, and debt. Value should include appropriate taxes, penalties, and fees.

❏ Consider using a QDRO specialist to divide any qualified retirement plans so funds aren't wasted on taxes or penalties.

❏ Close joint credit cards and other joint debt accounts. Lenders will come after you for joint debt when your spouse does not pay, which will harm your credit score. So think ahead about your credit score and financial security.

❏ Require in the decree for debt to be paid off using other assets. If that's not possible, ask to continue to receive statements and other documentation about joint debt that your spouse is required to pay. Be sure your settlement provides remedies when your ex doesn't pay.

10

Benefits and Insurance

WHILE MANY DIVORCING SPOUSES FOCUS ON retirement plans like 401(k)s, they fail to address other employee benefits. These include vacation pay and sick leave, of course, but also bonuses, health insurance, life insurance, disability insurance, stock options, restricted stock, deferred compensation plans, and pension benefits. Benefits might also include a company car, housing allowance, entertainment expenses, club memberships, frequent flyer miles, and even access to a company airplane.

Divorcing couples should consider the value benefit plans offer and have a strategy to replace important benefits, like health insurance, immediately after they sign the final decree.

Below, I've highlighted several valuable but often overlooked benefits.

Pension Benefits

"She can keep her pension. We'll divide everything else." I often hear this, and I wish I didn't. Pension benefits last a lifetime, and even a small monthly benefit can be valuable. The balance shown on a pension benefit statement is sometimes well below its actual value.

Joan and Tom

Fifty-year-old Joan had worked at the local university as head of the Anthropology Department since 2005. She married Tom, a handsome Neanderthal, in 2010. Five years later, they decided to divorce. (He wasn't evolving quickly enough.) Because the marriage was relatively short and the cost to analyze Joan's pension was $3,000, Tom told his attorney to ignore Joan's pension benefits. That was a mistake he came to rue. Because Tom was married to Joan for half of the time she accrued pension benefits, he might have received half of half (25 percent) of her total benefits. The value of her pension was close to $250,000. Tom may have given up a legal right to more than $60,000. Knowing Tom, he probably would have blown it all on a Budweiser-themed man cave, but that's not the point.

Pension benefits are based on average salaries and years of service. They don't start immediately upon employment but vest over time. If vesting happens during the marriage, all or portion of the pension could be considered a marital asset. For example, an employee might receive a pension equal to 2 percent of his salary multiplied by his years of service at the company, but only after five years of service. If he leaves the company after only four years, there is no benefit.

While nonvested pensions have no value if the employee spouse leaves the employer before he or she is fully vested, they may develop value in the future if the employee stays. The attorney for the nonemployee spouse may ask for a division of any future distribution (vested or not), if there is any, depending on state law. This is called the *deferred distribution method.* The non-employee spouse's percentage share depends on things like the length of the marriage or any joint contributions to the plan.

For a vested plan, you may be able to use the *offset method of distribution*, which allows you to exchange the value of the plan for other money available to the marital estate. This method will require an informal or formal appraisal of pension benefits to determine its value.

The division of a pension benefit requires a Qualified Domestic Relations Order, or QDRO (as defined in the previous chapter). Like other benefits, each state has its own rules regarding whether and how much of any pension benefit is marital property.

Financial analysts may use a *coverture fraction* calculation to divide pension benefits. For example, if you were married for ten years but your spouse accrued benefits over fifteen years, the marital portion would be two-thirds of the benefit (ten out of fifteen) and you would be eligible for half of that.

Typically the nonemployee spouse is the one who needs access to information about the employee spouse's pension plan. The nonemployee spouse may be able to get a form from the pension plan administrator that, with a signature from the employee, allows the nonemployee spouse to discuss the pension plan's terms and benefits.

While your attorney can prepare the QDRO, consider using a QDRO specialist with experience dividing pension plans in your state. Pension plans are complex. As described in chapter nine, a QDRO specialist is typically an experienced attorney who, along with the help of a financial planner or CDFA®, can sort through the best options to divide and value the plan, based on the plan's unique terms and your needs.

Stock Options

A stock option is a right to purchase stock at an agreed price upon exercise of the option. The *exercise* is permitted once the stock option vests, meaning it has been granted for a time sufficient enough for the right to be exercised. For example, a stock option might be granted in 2014 but it cannot be exercised until 2017. Hopefully, over the three years in between, the stock's value grows to exceed the agreed-upon price. If the agreed-upon price was $10 and the stock increases to $30, the stock option's owner will purchase the stock at $10, sell at the market price of $30, and earn $20.

The value of a stock option is often calculated using a complicated formula called the Black Scholes model (not as mysterious as black holes, but almost). Many plans do not allow an employee to transfer ownership of these benefits to a nonemployee spouse, but the value may be divided in divorce. Furthermore, an executive employee may be restricted from exercising options during the company's blackout periods (right before the company's earnings are announced, for example). Or the executive might be allowed to sell only according to a predetermined schedule (as part of the Securities and Exchange Commission's rules to prevent trading on inside information).

Taxes on options vary depending on the type of stock option plan. It's tricky, but it's important, because the way an option is taxed impacts its value. Review any proposed division with your CPA or tax preparer before agreeing to a final settlement.

Restricted stock is a similar benefit. Restricted stock is stock awarded based on time of service or other requirements. The value is often taxed like a bonus payment based on the value of the stock when it vests.

Dealing with stock options or restricted stock may involve extensive research and the input of financial experts and appraisers. However, like pensions, these benefits may have considerable value worth the time and expense to properly divide them. You don't need Stephen Hawking or Neil deGrasse Tyson, but you need an expert with the power to navigate around the black holes, fields of meteorites, and space garbage of these benefits.

Insurance

You should evaluate all available insurance to make sure you have adequate protection for you and the assets you may receive in the divorce, sometimes before you even know the outcome of negotiations. Insurance protects us from significant economic loss, but only when premium payments are up to date. There's insurance that protects your property, like homeowners insurance or automobile insurance, and there's insurance that can protect you and your income, like life, health, disability, and long-term care insurance. Start with a good understanding of each policy you already have. Make sure new policies and beneficiaries are established as quickly as possible after the final decree is signed. And make sure your spouse is required to continue his or her insurance, especially life insurance, if you or your children will depend on that spouse for support.

Life and Disability Insurance

Many employers offer group life and disability benefits. If your income will depend on child and/or spousal support, you may want the divorce decree to include life and disability insurance with benefits payable to you or to your children. The following examples demonstrate why.

Mari and Joe

Mari divorced her husband Joe, a successful architect. He agreed to pay child support and alimony for five years. Joe remarried quickly after their divorce. A year later he was in a car accident. After months of rehabilitation, Joe died. His new wife was the beneficiary of his life insurance policy and retirement plan at work. Mari was left with no support.

If the divorce decree had specified that Mari and the children be named as beneficiaries, their support payments might have been protected. The amount of life and disability insurance should be enough to protect support payments and should not depend on continued employment.

Debra and Tom

Debra and Tom divorced last year. Debra got custody of the children and child support from Tom. At the time of the divorce, Tom worked for a large corporation that provided a life insurance benefit two times his salary. A month after the divorce, Tom left his job to invest in a local start-up. Six months later, Tom died after hitting his head in a skiing accident.

Like Mari, Debra and her children ended up with much less money to support themselves. Tom's insurance depended on a job he no longer held. Debra and her attorney should have insisted (and required in the decree) that Tom purchase life and disability insurance that didn't depend on Tom's current employment alone. Or Debra could have negotiated that she be able to purchase life insurance on Tom's life in an amount sufficient to cover support. Depending on Tom's age and health, the benefits of this insurance might well outweigh the expense.

Abby and Nick

Abby and Nick divorced. In their settlement agreement, Abby agreed to pay Nick support payments for eight years. The agreement required Abby to purchase life insurance with Nick as the beneficiary in an amount sufficient to cover the payments. But Nick knew Abby all too well. Nick asked Abby to provide proof that she made the required monthly premium payments. As he'd predicted, Abby stopped making payments just six months after the divorce. He resumed the payments himself, and it's a good thing he did: Abby died a year later in a tragic car accident.

Life insurance is a complicated but necessary tool to protect support payments. Consult with a knowledgable agent or attorney about your options before negotiating your settlement. If your income depends on support, be sure that required life insurance premiums are paid, even if you have to pay them.

Health Insurance

Once you file for divorce, a spouse typically cannot be removed from his or her spouse's corporate health insurance plan until the divorce is final. Figure out your future coverage *before you finalize your settlement.* Once divorced, you generally cannot stay on your ex's health insurance.

If you've been covered by your spouse's employer plan, you may have an option to continue that health care under COBRA (the Consolidated Omnibus Budget Reconciliation Act). COBRA continues benefits for workers' families for limited periods under certain circumstances like voluntary or involuntary job loss. In divorce, an ex-spouse's group plan may offer the nonemployee spouse up to thirty-six months of coverage through COBRA if you apply almost immediately after you sign divorce papers (you have sixty days, but these rules can change).

Although costs might be higher, COBRA coverage may be better than coverage under the Affordable Health Care Act (ACA or ObamaCare), which is another option, for now. Depending on your postdivorce income, however, you may qualify for a subsidized plan through ObamaCare. Furthermore, like job loss, divorce is a life change that opens enrollment for you under the Affordable Health Care Act, but you need to enroll almost immediately after you sign your settlement. If you miss the window, you'll have to wait until open enrollment, which could be months away.

Until recently, advisors recommended that spouses who leave their partner's employer plan get their own individual plans. Advisors worried that if a spouse was on COBRA and then developed a preexisting condition, it would be difficult to get an independent plan. Now, preexisting conditions are covered under current health care law, but I still recommend that you consider a plan outside of your ex-spouse's employer plan. Health care legislation can change.

Your children can and probably should stay on the employee's plan (although you'll probably have to negotiate who pays the premiums). If both you and your spouse have a plan at work, you've probably already decided which of you will provide coverage for the children. If you and your children are covered under your spouse's plan, it's more likely that the settlement will require your spouse to continue to cover the children. Divorcing spouses should have a plan to replace coverage in case of job loss after divorce.

One last, and very important, note about postdivorce health insurance expenses for children. Responsibility for unreimbursed health care costs (deductibles, uncovered costs etc.) is often divided between the spouses in the decree. In fact, state law may require these expenses be divided. But health care providers won't care what your decree says. If you brought the child to a health care facility, the bill after reimbursements will likely go to you.

Marlene

Marlene had a car accident. Her thirteen-year-old daughter was injured in the accident. The unreimbursed hospital bill (after her car and health insurance paid their share) totaled $3,000. Marlene's divorce decree said that health care expenses would be divided between her and her ex-spouse. Marlene's ex, Mark, refused to pay. Mark told Marlene that the accident was her fault so she should be the one to pay medical costs.

If, as in Marlene's case, your ex won't pay, you may have to go back to your attorney or court to enforce the decree.

Property Insurance

Some insurance companies will look for nearly any excuse not to pay a claim, so update auto and homeowners insurance as soon as possible after the divorce is final. In fact, make your insurance agent aware of any anticipated change, including your change of address and/or where you will be living, once you know which cars and homes (or other insurable assets) will be your responsibility after the divorce. Contact the agent again, once title and deed transfers are complete.

What About Social Security Benefits?

Social Security houses several programs that provide benefits for unemployment, disability, temporary assistance, health care (Medicare for the aged and disabled, and Medicaid for low-income families), and other situations, but when people refer to "Social Security," they generally mean federal retirement benefits.

Social Security payments to retirees are funded by payroll taxes as a percentage of wages (12.4 percent of earnings up to the first $128,400 of earnings in 2018, half from the wage earner and half from the employer). These taxes are paid into the Social Security Trust Fund, which is administered by the US Treasury.

In order to be eligible for retirement benefits, you must earn credits. In 2018, you receive one credit for each $1,320 of earnings, up to the maximum of four credits per year. You need forty credits to be eligible, and your total benefit is based on your previous income. Certain government jobs have their own similar programs that reduce traditional Social Security benefits—and complicate what you may be eligible for in retirement postdivorce. And, like other benefits, the terms can change. For retirees, the normal retirement age creeps up periodically and the growth in payments has slowed. You can see your own credit and estimated benefits at www.ssa.gov.

For someone who is fifty years old today, the normal retirement age (NRA) is sixty-seven. Early retirement benefits start at sixty-two, but the benefit is greatly reduced for the remainder of your life (70 percent of normal retirement-age benefits). Those who are sixty-two and older will fare better working or using investments to support themselves until normal retirement age or later, as payments increase the longer you wait to take the benefit.

In divorce, these benefits are not divided. You are eligible for the greater of your own benefit or half of your spouse's (100 percent if your spouse is decreased) but only if you are sixty-two (reduced benefits), were married for ten years, and you are currently single. If you remarry, you lose the benefit until you divorce spouse number two. Taking benefits based on your ex's earnings record doesn't reduce your ex's benefit. In fact, he or she may not know that you are taking benefits based on their earnings record.

For ex-spouses with a limited work history, this benefit can be valuable, even life saving. Strategies to maximize benefits are a moving target. Every situation is unique and rules change. Before you proceed, seek out a Social Security specialist or go to www.ssa.gov to find out more.

Final Thoughts

Before signing a final divorce decree, consider the value and protection offered by employer benefit and insurance plans. These benefits, like investments, are more complicated than ever. It's often worth the expense to hire a specialist to analyze your and your spouse's benefit packages.

Action Items

❏ Have a plan in place that will replace important benefits and insurance, like health insurance, once you're divorced.

❏ Spend the time and money and get the expertise it takes to fully analyze complex benefits such as vacation pay, pension plans, stock options, and restricted stock.

❏ Be sure your spouse is required to continue life and disability coverage that does not depend on employment at his or her existing firm—especially if you'll be receiving child or spousal support.

11

College Savings

IT'S ONE THING WHEN YOUR SPOUSE conspires with your children to conceal a birthday present from you until the big day. Quite another when your spouse uses your children's college or other savings plan to hide assets that could be divided in your divorce.

Most state laws do not consider college funding to be an obligation of parents or part of child support. Negotiating college savings or who will cover expenses while happily married may be difficult. Divorce just adds fuel to the fire. If a spouse agrees to pay for college as a contractual obligation in the divorce settlement agreement, he or she must pay for college under that contract even when the spouse loses a job or needs to cover other expenses such as his or her own retirement—unless the contract is successfully renegotiated. Thus, a spouse who agrees to pay may have turned a moral obligation into a legal one.

I have four points to make here: First, college savings plans and the rules that govern them change all the time. New plans come on the scene periodically and their terms may be more favorable. Second, what you and I think of as "college" will change by the time our young children attend, so it's tricky to figure out how much you'll need to save. Third, and unfortunately, college savings plans as they exist today can serve as a means to hide assets from a spouse. For example, if your spouse recently added money to your children's UTMA or UGMA accounts, you may be left with less cash to divide upon divorce because those accounts can only be used for the benefit of or transferred to your children. Fourth, parents or their children can borrow money for college but they cannot borrow for their own retirement. Financial planners commonly remind clients to be sure their own projected retirement expenses are covered before they decide to help pay for college.

UGMA and UTMA Accounts

The Uniform Gift to Minors and Uniform Transfers to Minors Acts accounts (UGMA and UTMA) are custodial accounts for the benefit of the child. Anybody—close friend, aunt, or grandparent—can establish one of these accounts for a child. There are no contribution limits or deadlines. Depending on the state where the account is held, these accounts become property of the child at age eighteen or twenty-one (possibly later if defined by the custodian). The transfers are an irrevocable gift to the child. This means it is not possible to transfer money back to the custodian or parent from a child's UGMA or UTMA account.

UGMA and UTMA accounts were sometimes set up to reduce overall taxes on family investment accounts, but that benefit has been largely reduced by changes in tax law. These accounts are taxed, to a point, at the child's tax rate. Funds in these accounts are used for education or *any* purpose that benefits the child. However, unlike Section 529 plans and Coverdell Educational Savings Accounts (ESAs), you cannot transfer the account to another child or change beneficiaries. (I didn't say it was easy money.)

Nothing prevents the custodian from spending the money for the benefit of the child, so long as the expenses aren't parental obligations and they don't benefit the custodian. Parental obligations are expenses a parent is normally expected to provide—food, clothing, medical care, and shelter. The rules for UGMAs and UTMAs are state specific, so check your state's rules online.

UTMAs and UGMAs are great places to hide assets from a soon-to-be ex because you can't "take back" investments in these accounts. Why ? Because the UTMA or UGMA transfers to the child typically at the age of majority in your state—skipping directly to children (although they might not even know about it). In divorce, you or your attorney may be able to negotiate limits on the use of money from these accounts. But that may be about all that can be done without further (and expensive) legal action needed to prove that these accounts were set up primarily to deplete marital assets.

Tiffany

During her divorce, Tiffany shared with me a list of her family's assets. Tiffany thought that her husband was saving too much in their children's accounts and that she would be left with almost nothing in retirement. The children's accounts included two large UTMA accounts for her fourteen-year-old twin girls. Tiffany said that the girls attend private school and both are likely to receive academic scholarships. In mediation, Tiffany's attorney was able to help her negotiate that the UTMAs be used to pay for private school and college costs until they are depleted. Any excess would be distributed to the girls. Further, Tiffany asked to have online access to these accounts as well as copies of annual account statements.

In fact, all parents, whether divorcing or not, may consider spending down UTMA and UGMA accounts during their children's teen years on nonparental obligation expenses that benefit the child, such as private school. This is especially important if the child's ability to manage money at such a young age is in question.

Tips for UGMA and UTMA Accounts in Divorce:

- Review the terms of the account with the account's bank or investment company. Consult state rules and the plan provider before making any changes.
- In divorce, you'll want to negotiate whether to (or who will) continue to contribute to savings in these accounts

and whether to spend down these accounts by using the money for your child's K–12 schooling, higher education, or other specific nonparental support obligations before the age of majority.

- In divorce, the agreement could require that both the custodial and noncustodial parent have access to statements for the account.

Educational IRAs and Coverdell Education Savings Accounts

Educational IRAs and Coverdell Education Savings Accounts can be used for qualified education expenses, including K–12 and higher education expenses. Contributions go into an account that will eventually go to the beneficiary (child) if proceeds are not used for college.

Coverdell contributions are nondeductible and limited to $2,000 per year until the child is 18. Balances can transfer to another child. Distributions that are not used for qualified expenses incur taxes and a 10 percent penalty on gains to the beneficiary (child). The account must be fully withdrawn by the time the beneficiary reaches age thirty, or distributed to the beneficiary, and may be subject to penalties and taxes at the beneficiary's rate. These rules and limitations are subject to change. Work with the account provider or a CDFA® before negotiations to fully understand your options.

The beneficiary may not need or use all the contributions and gains for qualified expenses. As of this writing, any penalty is waived if the beneficiary is awarded a qualified scholarship, as defined by the account, or dies.

Tips for Educational IRAs and Coverdell Education Savings Accounts in Divorce

- Review the terms of the account with the account's bank or investment company. Consult the plan provider before making any changes.

- In divorce, you'll want to negotiate whether to (or who will) continue to contribute to savings in these accounts and whether to spend down these accounts by using the money for your child's education or to transfer the benefit to another family member.

Section 529 College Savings Plans

Section 529 College Savings Plans can be used for qualified higher education expenses and, for now, up to $10,000 per year of K-12 private school. Like Coverdell accounts, 529 plans are transferrable to another family member and penalties are waived for withdrawals not needed for education when the child receives a scholarship or dies. Unlike Coverdell accounts, 529 plans have larger contribution limits. Unlike UTMA and UGMA custodial accounts, which belong to the beneficiary child and cannot be taken back, 529 plans can be distributed to the parents in divorce or otherwise, although withdrawal for nonqualified expenses (meaning any distribution to the parents) will incur taxes and penalties, but only on investment growth.

This is an important distinction in divorce, especially if the beneficiary does not pursue higher education or qualified expenses are less than the amount saved in the plan. These accounts can be awarded to either or both parents in divorce if they need postdivorce liquidity (cash), but taxes and penalties apply.

Rita and Roger

Rita and Roger started a 529 plan when their son Jimmy was only six years old. In the divorce settlement agreement, Roger was the named custodian on the account. Rita wanted to have online access to these accounts as well as copies of annual account statements so she could be sure that the savings were used for Jimmy's college education. The agreement did not require that funds only be used for Jimmy's education or include what the couple would do if Jimmy didn't need money for qualified college expenses. Years later, Jimmy was a star athlete with several colleges vying for his attention. It turned out Jimmy didn't need the money for college. That was covered by the coach. Four years later, Rita got a copy of the 529 plan account statement. There was nothing left in it. Roger took the money to buy a new Porsche. Roger said he bought the car for Jimmy, but Facebook photos always showed Roger at the wheel. He bought the car for himself! There was nothing she could do except return to court.

Just because 529 withdrawals must be used for qualified expenses, that doesn't mean there won't be non-qualified withdrawals. Rita could have negotiated that the funds were only to be used in the interest of the beneficiary. Or she could have asked for the account to be divided so that she would be in control of her share. Like Heather in chapter five, Rita could have negotiated for the unused portion of this money during settlement negotiations, but she didn't know this was an option. Again, when one of the spouses needs cash to start life over again, it may be worth it to withdraw and divide these accounts as part of the divorce, despite paying penalties and taxes on the investment growth.

Tips for 529 Plans in Divorce

- Review the terms of the account with the account provider. Identify the custodian, who may not be one of the parents. Consult the plan provider before making any changes.

- In divorce, you'll want to negotiate whether to (or who will) continue to contribute to savings in these accounts and how to divide nonqualified distributions

- *Consider these accounts a source of cash.* Financial planners typically advise that clients save for retirement first, then college for their children. If other postdivorce cash is insufficient to support the basic needs of parents, you may want to withdraw the net amount after taxes and penalties.

Financial Aid and Student Loans

College funding may include student loans from various federal and private programs. Like college savings programs, loan programs change often. Go to www.savingforcollege.com for a resource guide to these programs.

Maximizing access to low-cost student loans is complex and may require the assistance of a financial planner or college aid specialist. According to www.savingforcollege.com at the time of this writing, the formula for determining family contributions is based more on income than on assets and more on the student's income and assets than the parents'. After divorce, one parent often has a much lower income. For now, generally speaking, the custodial parent with the lower income should apply for federal student loans, although this could change. Eligibility is based on a review of the parent's Free Application for Federal Student Aid (FAFSA), which considers both the student's and parents' income.

The assets and income that count will impact access to low-cost student loans. Equity in your primary home and retirement plans don't count. UGMA and UTMA accounts count as student assets and may increase a student's income due to interest and dividends from those accounts. Parents may be able to convert UGMA and UTMA accounts to 529 plans under specific rules, which may reduce reported resources. For now, a small portion of 529s count as a family contribution, but only if the parent is the owner (custodian). Grandparent owners of 529s do not count. A 529 account or ESA owned by a dependent student, or by a custodian for the student, does not have to be included with other student-owned investments. These accounts are reported on the federal aid application (FAFSA) as parental assets.

Got it? Probably not. I'm overwhelmed by the Byzantine

nature of this application. And just when all of us think we have a handle on it, it will change.

Final Thoughts

When properly negotiated with both spouses' interests in mind, college planning shouldn't have to derail your divorce or your financial planning goals.

Saving and allocating savings for college is already complicated. Parents often disagree about how much to save or spend on their children's education. In divorce, it's even worse. If you want to live frugally while Junior goes to college but your spouse doesn't, it's difficult in most states to negotiate an agreed-upon commitment.

College starts just when parental obligations end. Although judges in a few states can order a parent to commit to covering college costs, you and your spouse should attempt to work it out on your own, without the court's involvement. A legal commitment could subject you to additional court fights and may even derail your own support and retirement.

Action Items

❑ Consult with the plan sponsor or bank before you agree to any changes because rules for custody, withdrawal contributions, taxes, and the impact on borrowing for college can change.

❏ Make sure both parents have access to account statements after divorce and, if possible, agree to divide any unused portion.

❏ For many parents a college education is a priority. However, funding that priority is even more challenging when one household becomes two. By adding a college funding commitment to a divorce decree, couples may unwittingly be turning a priority into a legal obligation to fund college even though they may struggle to meet their own basic needs.

❏ When postdivorce funds are insufficient to cover expenses, consider liquidating college plans. You can't borrow your way into retirement, but your children can borrow their way through college. Save yourself first. Then assist your child with his oxygen mask.

12.

Business Valuation

WHETHER THE BUSINESS IS ARTISANAL CHEESE or auto parts, dividing it gets, well, divisive. You don't want the twenty pounds of imported Limburger or fifty boxes of pistons, but you'll sure take the stacks of twenties in the bank deposit bag. We're talking money here, and pride, but mostly money.

Whether you own and/or operate a business or your spouse does, a business created or business interest purchased during the marriage is very likely marital property. It's also one of the largest and most contentious assets in divorce.

There are lots of questions: Should you co-own the business? Can you co-own the business? Should you sell the business and divide the money? Will you have to do so in order to survive financially? Or should you give up your share of the business in exchange for other financial assets? Before you make that decision, read this chapter so you can understand how businesses are valued generally, and in divorce.

How Much Is It Worth?

Below are three basic methods to value a business in divorce—liquidation, market, and capitalization.

Liquidation: Here, you look at the value of all the *tangible* assets, like stinky cheese and pistons. Unless business operations are obsolete and sales are way down, this method is unlikely to be appropriate. It yields the lowest value and is not appropriate for service businesses like law firms or doctors' practices.

Market: Using this method, the business value is either a multiple of revenue or cash flow (revenue less expenses) based on similar businesses that recently sold. For example, if a dry cleaning business in your area sold for two times its revenue, your dry cleaning business might also sell for two times its revenue. This method also can be used when the divorcing couple's business recently sold a portion of its operations to a new partner, but only if that sale was a true market sale and not an insider price. Valuation based on an *insider price* can be used as just another way to hide asset value. Did your spouse sell part of the business to a related party when he or she knew divorce was on the horizon? If so, was the price depressed to lower overall firm value?

Discounted cash flow or capitalization: This method uses cash flow, cash flow growth, and the regularity of cash flow to determine the value of a business. If you agree on the cash flow from your business (which may be adjusted for things like personal expenses or any unusual or one-time expenses), you may use this method, but you'll need to agree on assumptions about cash flow growth and cash flow certainty in the future. This is a common approach, but any change in the assumptions can greatly impact the result.

The trouble is these methods are only useful when willing buyers and sellers negotiate in good faith. Real buyers argue that a target business's cash flow is uncertain and growth is slowing in order to reduce the price they'll be willing to pay (buy low). Sellers argue that cash flow is secure and growing rapidly to inflate the price (sell high). Buyers and sellers negotiate somewhere in the middle. But divorce often means there is no willing buyer or seller, let alone good faith, so it gets tricky. For one thing, the spouse involved in the day-to-day operations of the business may understate the value of the business to reduce what he will pay to buy out the other spouse. He has an incentive to play down the value. If he was selling the business to a willing buyer, he would certainly argue for a higher price instead.

Bill and Brenda

Bill owns a business that sells specialty windshield wipers to luxury car companies and car owners. Bill and his wife Brenda decide to divorce. Bill tells Brenda he takes an $80,000 salary from the business each year and that he's recently thought about selling the business because sales are down. Bill's business broker says the business is worth only $150,000. Brenda smells a rat, or at least a nervous mouse. They live in a nice neighborhood, their children attend private schools, and they vacation in Europe twice a year. Where is all the money coming from?

If Bill offers Brenda a business valuation report of his own, Brenda and her Certified Divorce Financial Analyst should review the report together. They should review variables used to determine value and look into them. They may decide it's worth hiring their own qualified business valuation expert. If they do, they should look for someone with an ABV, AVA, or CVA designation. The ABV is the Accredited Business Valuation designation given to CPAs and issued by the American Institute of Certified Public Accountants. AVA is the Accredited Valuation Analyst designation (sometimes now called a CVA or Certified Valuation Analyst) issued by the National Association of Certified Valuation Analysts (NACVA).

This is a critical step in the divorce process. Avoid the temptation to save the fee, thinking you can just agree to a value. Avoid the mistake, too, of relying on business tax reviews. You and your financial advisor should review the business tax return, but remember that a return is structured to *minimize* income, and thus minimize taxes. Taxable income is different from business cash flow. A business valuation expert will add back some non-cash expenses to taxable income to get close to the average ongoing cash flow (cash revenue less cash expenses) used for valuation.

So how might Bill try to fudge on the value of his wiper business? He could do any of the following:

- Delay new sales contracts
- Increase inventory or change how inventory is valued

- Prepay expenses to reduce cash flow
- Hire new employees or pay friends or family members for "services" to reduce cash flow
- Prepay taxes or keep any tax refund on deposit with the IRS for the following year's taxes
- Sell a partnership interest in the business at below market value to a friend or family member to justify a lower value

Scenarios abound. Believe me, I've seen some creative moves, and they weren't on the dance floor. An appraiser is trained to quickly recognize creative moves (aka, a change in the business's patterns). If the owner is not forthcoming with financial or other information about the business, the opposing attorney could subpoena records, potentially revealing coveted private information.

If you are the business owner, here's my advice: cooperate. Your own "creative" moves or stalling will come back to haunt you like those ghosts in *A Christmas Carol*. Your spouse's valuation expert may quickly catch on, and it won't look so good to the mediator or judge. Even worse, the opposing attorney can ask the court to put the business into receivership. Don't let that happen. It'll ruin the value of the business for both you and your soon-to-be ex.

Additional Considerations

The court may also consider a company's *goodwill*, of which there are two types—personal and enterprise. Personal goodwill is just that. Clients come to the business owner for his particular services. Think of your hair stylist. He or she relies on significant goodwill, or trust in the quality of her services, for success. There is value to personal goodwill, and that value is personal—and in some states—not marital. Enterprise goodwill is associated with a service business that, for example, has a great location, or where changing ownership doesn't have as much impact on the business value (a burger franchise, for example). The degree of goodwill is debatable and the subject of many a courtroom drama. Whether and what type of goodwill is or is not included in the marital or community estate depends on the laws in your state.

You should also understand that if you or your spouse own less than a controlling interest or 50 percent of the business, the value of the business interest is discounted. The value is reduced bcause the ownership is less valuable when the owner can't make decisions on his or her own. There may also be a discount on marketability because there is no market—like the stock market—to easily trade the interest. These discounts can be steep, reducing the value by 35 percent or more.

And then there's the debt against the business. Debt is deducted from business value. Just like home equity, the value of the business to be divided is reduced by the debt owed. If your spouse says that the business is loading up on debt, you might want to question the purpose of that debt. This could be a red flag. If the debt was used to pay Uncle Freddy for "future auto parts," he or she may actually be trying to reduce business value by the amount of the debt. Once the divorce is over, Uncle Freddy just gives the cash back, the debt is gone, and you are left with much less than the real value of the business to divide—unless you go to court.

Let's face it: Divorce can be devastating to a business even if all parties are up front and honest. The owners are distracted and lenders may worry about the business's stability and the ability to pay. Both impact the success of the business.

Since there often is no willing buyer or seller in divorce, the valuation—based on subjective factors such as goodwill, controlling interest discounts, and debt—can vary widely. Typically, judges have to defer to the experts (and possibly split the difference), so make sure you have one fighting for your interests. The most difficult task is balancing the cost of a fight with the value you'll receive—win or lose.

Final Thoughts

Like retirement plans and pensions, dividing a business is complex. Because money can easily be "hidden" in a business, hiring a qualified valuation expert will save more than it costs—possibly much more.

Action Items

❏ Have a qualified expert value the business in your case. These experts will reveal any "tricks" your spouse may try and help you decide whether it's worth a fight in court. And don't use these tricks yourself. They could put you out of business.

❏ Have your advisor explain to you how changes to assumptions impact value.

13

Postdivorce Financial Planning

YOU'VE SIGNED YOUR SETTLEMENT AGREEMENT, BUT don't "settle" yet. There is still plenty to do. And you need to do it FAST. It's not about the elephant in the room anymore. It's about cheetahs and roadrunners and greyhounds and thoroughbred racehorses. In other words, get moving.

As soon as your divorce is final, consult with your attorney and financial analyst again. Understand all the terms of the divorce decree. I know you are tired of paying attorney fees, but it's critical that you get all questions answered now before the terms of the decree turn into a real problem.

Carrie

When Carrie divorced in 2012, she didn't understand the financial terms of her agreement. She felt overwhelmed, so she ignored it. Two years later, feeling a little braver, she

reviewed her settlement agreement. She learned that it pro-
vided her 60 percent of a $150,000 joint investment account
($90,000). That money would really help. Except it wouldn't.
It was now 2014 and the account was worth only $40,000.
What happened? Her ex-husband spent some of the money
and invested the rest in risky investment funds. Carrie was
left with only $24,000.

Carrie ended up back in court, fighting for something that was no longer there. It's important to *execute the changes required in the decree as soon as possible.* Hiring a financial planner or CDFA® postdivorce will help spur you to move quickly.

Investment Accounts

For joint bank accounts and investment accounts you'll have to provide the correct combination of signatures and documents that each bank requires in order to get your share. Your bank's website should have the requirements listed, but don't be surprised if these instructions are incomplete. Every account is unique. You may need to call or have your CDFA® call with you in order to understand what you need. Hopefully you did this before you signed your settlement agreement because if you waited until after, you may have to chase down your ex or the documents you need, wasting precious time and money in the process.

Typically one spouse will move his or her share of a joint account, and the other will change the name of the joint account to his or her own name. However, it's best practice to move each share of the account into a new individual account and close the joint account.

Retirement Accounts

Your attorney should file the proper documents to divide retirement accounts that require a QDRO like a 401(k) retirement plan or pension plan. Ask your attorney for a copy of the QDRO filing. For 401(k) plans, a QDRO moves the spouse's share to an Alternate Payee account. It's up to you to do the rest.

Joan

Joan was awarded half her husband's $200,000 401(k). She received paperwork in the mail telling her that her share was moved to an Alternate Payee account in her name. Joan wanted $30,000 from the account to make a down payment on a new home. However, the form from the 401(k) administration team only had two options: take all the money as cash or move the funds to an IRA. She was told that if she took all the money as cash, the plan administrator would withhold 20 percent for taxes and she would pay ordinary income taxes and penalties on the full account. Joan didn't want to buy the home right away, so she moved the account to an IRA at her bank and, two years later, withdrew $30,000. Joan was taxed on the withdrawal and also paid a 10 percent ($3,000) penalty.

Could Joan have avoided the penalty? Possibly. Had she spoken to a knowledgeable attorney, account administrator, or experienced financial analyst before taking a partial withdrawal, she might have avoided $3,000 in penalties.

As noted back in chapter nine, some retirement plans, such as IRAs, may not require a QDRO in order to be divided. However, like other investment accounts, the bank or investment firm may require a verifiable form of the decree as well as specific protocols, forms, and signatures to divide these accounts. If any of these weren't signed by your ex by now, unfortunately you'll need to wait to get his or her signature before dividing accounts.

Credit Cards and Bank Accounts

Close all joint credit cards and ensure that your former spouse's name is no longer on your account as an authorized user, unless you'll need the additional credit *and* your ex-spouse is trustworthy. It's tempting to hang onto a joint credit card. Who knows whether you'll be able to get as much (or any) credit on your own? But there is no such thing as joint credit. If your spouse uses the card and fails to pay, you'll get stuck with the bill. If you don't pay, your credit rating will suffer, making it even more difficult to get credit.

If you haven't already, open a credit card in your own name and begin to establish credit. If your financial status won't allow for this, consider starting with a secured credit card from your bank to build your credit.

Last, if possible, set up a separate bank checking or savings account in your name with six to nine months of anticipated expenses. This will serve as your emergency fund.

Health and Other Insurance

If you haven't already, revise your health insurance coverage as soon as possible. Let your company know immediately who needs coverage and who does not. For nonworking spouses, apply for individual coverage, or coverage under COBRA, or the Affordable Health Care Act. Divorce is a change that allows you to apply outside of ACA open enrollment periods, but you must move quickly to take advantage of this accommodation.

Update your auto, home, renters, and any other insurance with your new address.

Taxes

Your tax advisor needs a copy of your decree in order to prepare your taxes. For example, the decree instructs the advisor as to who will take child exemptions or tax credits and whether to file as single or head of household.

If you and your ex-spouse can cooperate, use the same tax advisor to prepare your taxes individually as prescribed in the decree with the goal of reducing your combined taxes. If you choose the *lowest taxes* method, your tax advisor can help you share the benefits of filing that way.

Estate Plans, Wills, and Beneficiaries

Change the beneficiaries on all your life insurance policies and retirement plans (401(k)s, pension plans, and IRAs). If your spouse was the beneficiary of any bank or investment accounts, change those, too.

Execute a new will and amend any trusts. You may need a new guardian or contingent guardian for your children, particularly for financial issues.

Changing Your Name and Other Updates

You may want to wait until all accounts and property that were awarded to you are in your own name before changing your name. Then, contact the Social Security Administration and obtain a new driver's license. If necessary, change car titles with your Department of Motor Vehicles. Your attorney or his or her paralegal can help you change your name if you're feeling uneasy about all of this.

Documents to Have and to Hold

After your divorce, prepare a binder with pockets for identity (birth certificates, marital certificates, Social Security cards, passports, car titles, deeds, copies of driver's licenses) as well as evidence of new accounts, insurance, the divorce agreement, taxes, and estate planning documents. This will smooth the transition for you and your children.

Keep recent joint tax returns, brokerage statements, bank statements, and mortgage statements, too. If you have young children, keep copies of their most important documents (as listed above) as well as immunization records and a list of doctors.

Last, retain receipts (or copies of online evidence) for any child support payments or spousal support (alimony) payments. Keep copies of all checks paid by you to, or received by you from, your former spouse.

Now What? Investing with New Goals in Mind

Now that you've organized your financial separation, what's next? How can you get your financial plan back on track?

First, understand your income and expenses. There's a budgeting template on my website. If you don't know your income and expenses, sort these out quickly because you'll need to reassess your investment and retirement plans. The portfolio you had as a couple may no longer fit. Do you need to reduce risk or increase income from the account?

When you have enough money to cover expenses for at least six to nine months, consider investing. If you have excess funds or retirement plans, get a proposal from a qualified investment advisor.

Now that you are on your own, explore your financial future. Do you want to save for a car, a new home, or college? How do you plan to live in retirement? Do you need to explore disability or long-term care insurance?

Many divorce financial analysts (CDFA®s) offer financial planning and investment services postdivorce, but others do not. Referrals from friends, coworkers, or other professionals are a great place to start. What do they like about the advisor? How long have they worked with the advisor? How often do they meet? What topics are covered at the meetings? Who calls the meetings? How responsive is the advisor to requests for service? Next, check the firm's website and read your prospective advisor's biography. What designations do they have? One prominent designation is the Certified Financial Planner (CFP®) designation (www.cfp.net and www.letsmakeaplan.org). These professionals pass a rigorous exam, have at least three years' experience, and complete ongoing education.

The transition to investing after divorce can be particularly overwhelming for the spouse who has never invested money before. More often than not, this is the wife or stay-at-home mom. The biggest mistake may be not investing at all. Of all assets controlled by women 71 percent are held in cash according to a study by an investment firm called BlackRock. When you leave your savings in cash, you may miss out on market gains that could be earned over the long run, and even worse, your cash will be less valuable due to inflation. Inaction will actually lessen your purchasing power and your ability to support yourself going forward.

Is Your Advisor Compliant with Regulations?

Several governmental and professional organizations regulate the activities of financial advisors. To check to see if your potential advisor has any prior or pending legal actions or complaints, look up a potential advisor on the Financial Industry Regulatory Authority's (FINRA's) Broker Check website (visit brokercheck.finra.org), your state's Department of Insurance, or www.CFP.net. If the initial review goes well, the next step is to prepare yourself for your first meeting with the advisor.

Is Your Advisor Listening?

Make sure your advisor has a clear picture of your current financial situation, your attitude toward investment risk, and your financial goals—both the essentials, like saving for retirement or college, and the dreams, like owning your own business. Next, prepare to share all the documents you gathered in chapter three and your divorce settlement agreement. Then, start listening. Consider whether the advisor's approach is too conservative or too aggressive for you. If possible, meet other members of the advisor's support team because you'll interact with the firm as well as the advisor.

Some financial advisors work alone, while others work as part of a team that includes other professionals (estate planning attorneys, CPAs, and tax professionals or insurance agents). Find out how these professionals are associated with the advisor and how they are compensated. You may want to get a list of their names to check their backgrounds as well.

What's This All Going to Cost?

Compensation and service offerings vary greatly. Understand the terms an advisor uses, like "fee only," which means that the advisor charges a flat or hourly fee. The advisor may charge a percentage of the investments, typically 1 percent or so, or collect commissions paid by the provider of the investment sold to you. Assume nothing. If fees are not clear or transparent to you, ask more questions. It is important to understand how your advisor is compensated and what services you should expect.

Is the advisor choosing investments that are best for his clients or best for his own pocketbook? While no single compensation model is right for everyone, I believe that interests are more aligned when the advisor is paid by the client (hourly fee or fees based on the amount you invest with the firm) and not by the investments the advisor chooses for his client (commissions, mainly).

How Can You Get Started?

Once you decide to engage an advisor, find out if you need to move accounts. Will you have to sell existing investments to make the transition? What will that cost? What is the tax consequence? Finally, understand your exit options. A potential advisor should walk you through your transition *to* the firm but should also explain how a potential transition *from* the firm occurs. When things don't work out, you don't want to be stuck with penalties or undisclosed fees. You'll want to be able to move to a new advisor quickly and without any drama.

Investments are complex, but you are smart and capable. The key to good investment management is transparency and education. Your advisor should explain the tools he or she uses to invest, such as stocks, bonds, mutual funds, and index funds. He or she should answer your questions and help you make an informed decision. If you've chosen well, your advisor will listen and answer your questions directly. If you hear: "I'll take care of it," or "You don't need to know the specifics," you may want to interview other potential advisors.

Engaging a financial advisor is not a license to ignore your financial obligations. You still must pay attention. This is your financial future, regardless of who is playing on your team.

Final Thoughts

Delaying decisions about your money and financial life contributes to anxiety and expensive trips back to the courtroom. Organizing your financial life can give you the confidence you need to begin your new single life or as a single parent.

Action Items

❏ Spend additional time (and money) to ask your attorney final questions you have about your agreement.

❏ Interview financial planners and CDFA®s right away to help you execute your agreement (find one at www.institutedfa.com). Dividing your resources quickly will save money and headaches in the long run.

❏ Keep organized. Start a financial planning notebook.

❏ Choose advisors who listen to your financial goals and are dedicated to helping you achieve them.

Final Thoughts—Finally!

MY HOPE IS THAT YOU PLOWED through every chapter in this book and now have more confidence and hope for whatever it is you are facing—cohabitation, an upcoming wedding, another year of a successful marriage, a trial separation, or divorce. Because money matters today are so complicated, I also hope this book leads you to the office of a brilliant and kind financial planner who specializes in relationships and divorce.

But ultimately, I hope that the ties that bind you from now on are only ties that you desire, that make you happy and whole. Thanks for reading, and I wish you the very best.

Index

About the Author

**PAM FRIEDMAN HAS OVER TWENTY-FIVE** years of financial planning and investment experience. Prior to partnering with Silicon Hills Wealth Management, LLC, Ms. Friedman was on Wall Street in both New York and London structuring and raising capital for both public and private companies. Upon her return to Texas, Ms. Friedman spent six years on the faculty of the Finance Department in the McCombs School of Business at The University of Texas at Austin.

Ms. Friedman assists men and women in identifying all the assets of the marriage, including those that potentially may be hidden or under reported. She also provides detailed projections that demonstrate how different financial settlements will impact the client's family for the short and long term. Lastly, Ms. Friedman helps ensure that other financial areas are addressed such as life insurance, beneficiaries, estate and college planning.

Ms. Friedman earned the designation Certified Financial Planner™ (CFP®) in 2006 and Certified Divorce Financial Analyst® (CDFA®) in 2011. Pam is also a trained family law mediator. Pam holds an MBA, BBA, and BA in Finance and Economics from The University of Texas at Austin.

Pam married her husband Mitch in 2014. They chose to negotiate a pre-marital agreement. And it has been amended, twice.

Made in the USA
Las Vegas, NV
21 February 2022

44322217R00125